INDICATIONS OF A MYSTERIOUS PATH

Indications of a MYSTERIOUS PATH

— A MEMOIR

RONALD LUTZ

LUMINARE PRESS
WWW.LUMINAREPRESS.COM

Indications of a Mysterious Path: A Memoir
Copyright © 2022 by Ronald Lutz

All rights reserved. This book or any portion thereof may not be reproduced or used in any manner whatsoever without the express written permission of the publisher, except for the use of brief quotations in a book review.

Printed in the United States of America

Luminare Press
442 Charnelton St.
Eugene, OR 97401
www.luminarepress.com

LCCN: 2022903869
ISBN: 978-1-64388-960-3

*Dedicated to my relatives,
friends, and neighbors.*

A NOTE FROM THE AUTHOR

I had written a novel but could not think of anything else to write until the nephew of my partner suggested I write about my life so that he could get to know me better. I shrugged off his suggestion at first, but remembrances and experiences kept creeping into my mind until I finally decided to put them down on paper. I did not write much about the many happy and humorous occurrences in my life; they are difficult to recapture on paper. Because of that, the prose is more purposeful and cannot be confused with light entertainment.

I started to write this memoir using a pseudonym but one of my friends said he disliked reading first-person accounts, and I came to dislike writing in that narrative as well. With that in mind, I replaced the first-person "I" with the third-person "Ron," and dropped the fictitious author's name.

I am not a celebrity, politician, member of royalty or—except to maybe a few people—a person of controversy. So, as another friend of mine said, paraphrasing a famous politician, "they can read it if they want to and not read it if they don't want to."

*For it is not the one who commends himself
who is approved,
but the one whom the Lord commends.*

2 CORINTHIANS 10:18

INTRODUCTION

Raised in a rural Ohio family, Ronald was blessed to have parents who provided him with food, clothes, and comfort, and enabled him to tour the world. But as an adult, he was troubled by the use of alcohol and drugs, affected by mental illness, and possibly touched by the Holy Spirit. He would be the first to tell you his contributions to society are minimal. Not a social person, he managed to graduate from college, served in the army, and then worked in manufacturing a short time. Disillusioned by the direction of his life he joined the Peace Corps. Fourteen months in Malaysia preceded a move to California and a job in Yosemite National Park before moving to San Diego. Eventually he entered a Christian rehabilitation program, and several years later returned to work in Ohio and met a woman who was honest, practical, and affectionate. They developed a relationship and toured the world while he was still learning to recognize indications of a mysterious path.

CHAPTER 1
1947-1952

When he grew older, Ron learned that nine months after his father and mother were married, the Japanese attacked Pearl Harbor, thrusting the United States into World War II. The next year his parents moved to Springfield, Missouri, where his father served the duration of the war as an army hospital nurse because of restricted eyesight. Their marriage spanned fifty-five years and produced two children. His sister was born in Springfield in May 1944.

His father and mother had been raised in an exclusively white, rural farm area near Bucyrus, Ohio, and graduated from the same rural school. His mother was three years older than his father, but he knew her because she was the sister of one of his best classmate friends. His father was twenty and worked at a farm-related job when they married; his mother was twenty-three and clerked in a city office. Then his father was conscripted to serve in the army. When the war ended, they returned to Ohio and reacquainted themselves to the community. His mother visited relatives in Akron occasionally, shopping with them or going to movies; she joined them at Garfield High School baseball games and became a fan of a few players on the team. She liked one of their pitchers so much that he became Ron's namesake. Ronald Negray eventually made it to the Major Leagues and pitched for several years.

His mother gave birth to Ronald Clifford Lutz, a five--pound, six-ounce baby boy at the Bucyrus hospital in January 1947. His birth preceded some other notable events of that year. In February the French incursion at the battle of Hanoi initiated the first Indo-China war that eventually led to the United States' involvement in Vietnam. In April, black player Jackie Robinson, from the Kansas City Monarchs of the Negro League, broke Major League Baseball's color barrier when he played for the National League's Brooklyn Dodgers after signing a contract two years earlier with Branch Rickey, an Ohio native and graduate of Ohio Wesleyan College in Delaware. (Three months later Larry Doby broke the color barrier in the American League when he signed a contract and played with the Cleveland Indians.) George Marshall announced his plan for economic aid to war-torn Europe in June, the same month *The Diary of Anne Frank* was published; in July the ship Exodus 1947 carried the largest illegal number of Jewish refugees from displaced camps in Europe to Palestine; in August both Pakistan and India gained independence from British rule; and in November, Princess Elizabeth married Lieutenant Philip Mountbatten.

The year after his birth his parents moved to a new home, renting a 240-acre farm south of Bucyrus in Crawford County. His father grew up on a farm and loved farming; his mother loved music. She occasionally played piano and the organ at church, and in later years gave lessons to neighboring kids, but after moving to the farm with two young children to raise she assumed the full-time role of housewife. Besides farming the land, his father raised beef cattle, hogs and, sometime later, sheep. Chickens were raised in a coop near the house and his mother visited it every day to get the hens' eggs. They also had a large vegetable garden and the farm had an established apple tree orchard. His parents were attentive to all the responsibilities and enjoyed all the comforts of life on the farm.

The day after Ron's first birthday, Mahatma Gandhi was assassinated. In May, Israel declared itself an independent state. In October, unbeknownst to him, the Cleveland Indians baseball team won the World Series over the Boston Braves. He would become a lifelong fan of the Cleveland team, but as of the year 2021 its last championship was the 1948 season. In November,

Harry Truman defeated Thomas Dewey in a contested presidential election in which a Chicago paper headline declared Dewey the winner. These events were not apparent to him at his early age as were any recollections of bad experiences during his nurturing or formative years. He did hear rumors of his mother's long depression after his birth; his Aunt Florence told him she cared for him while his mother recovered. But as much as he can remember, it must have been a loving, caring, and secure time for him and his sister. His parents gave them a real sense of who they were. In his case, however, their instruction did not prepare him for when it was time to leave their home.

Technological developments were at the forefront of life in the United States about the time of his second birthday. The first television broadcast connecting the East Coast to Midwest stations occurred and would soon allow audiences to view programming that included the *Texaco Star Theater* hosted by Milton Berle and the stringed puppet of *The Howdy Doody Show* hosted by Buffalo Bob Smith. In March the first automatic street light was installed in New Milford, Connecticut, and three months later a V2 rocket carried the first monkey, Albert II, eighty-three miles into outer space. Unaware of these developments, the first childhood memory he recalled from that summer was when the landlady of the farm gifted a small cardboard box to the family in which rested a tiny, months-old fox terrier dog. She was brown with a white streak down the middle of her face and a white belly and feet; they called her Ginger.

Ginger, circa 1951

She was small enough to run between the legs of their other large dog, Bruno, to his apparent consternation. Bruno died a short time later due to old age.

The new decade brought new challenges for the United States. Communism had begun to flourish in other countries and the House Un-American Activities Commission, created in 1938 to investigate citizens alleged to be communist sympathizers, continued to hold hearings. The Soviet Union, China, and Korea were all flexing their muscles based on a communist ideology, and in June the onset of the Korean War was one of the results. A cold war mentality, pitting rival nation doctrines against one another was demonstrated in the United States with the testing of more V2 experimental rockets. In July, a Bumper rocket previously tested in New Mexico became the first rocket launch at Cape Canaveral in Florida. However, not all developments were attributed to the Cold War. July 1951 marked the first publication of J.D. Salinger's book *The Catcher in the Rye* and in September *I Love Lucy* premiered on CBS about the same time the first color television was available on the market. Ignorant of all these goings-on, his days on the farm were peaceful and included occasional parties held at his grandparents' home, the parents of his father; they lived in a large two-story house on a farm one mile north of the one rented by his parents. The grandest of their parties were all-day affairs and remain etched in his memory.

Guests began arriving in early afternoon. His grandparents entertained their adult children, including Ron's father, his mother, her parents and their other children, and numerous friends. A typical party lasted well past his bed time. A croquet court was set up on the lawn surrounding the house. The adjacent barnyard had enough space for a softball field and a badminton court. Large metal troughs used to water livestock were cleaned and filled with ice to cool beverages for the guests and outdoor grills were fired up to roast chicken, bratwursts and corn-on-the-cob. Twenty or thirty guests roamed the yard at any one time during the day; at night, strings of lights decorated the area and guests moved into the house to enjoy hot apple cider with homemade doughnuts and hand-cranked ice cream. They were wonderful, fond memories from his youth.

Significant events occurred the next year including Elizabeth II assuming the throne of Great Britain following her father's death; Bautista led a successful coup in Cuba; the first rock 'n' roll concert, the Moondog Coronation Ball, was held in Cleveland, Ohio; and the Kentucky Derby was televised for the first time. Even more important to Ron than these events and Eisenhower's election as president later that year was his first day in school. As his parents told him, a school administrator asked them if it would be okay for him to begin the first grade at the age of five—there was no kindergarten at that time—due to an expected large class the next year. They thought it would be okay. His sister was starting third grade; they were going to the same rural school their parents had attended. His father was driving the school bus to earn extra money; he began his route at their home so they were the first kids to get on the bus. Being the first boy on board, his father designated him flag boy; he remembers it as his first introduction to a form of responsibility. He was required to exit the bus at each house where kids were to be picked up; he walked in front of the bus and held out a red flag visible to vehicles that might be approaching from behind or in the opposite lane of traffic, warning them to halt so the children could safely cross the street and board the bus.

Only one time in the several years during his time as flag boy did a possible dangerous situation occur: a flatbed semi-truck approached the rear of the bus at high speed and had to brake hard in order to stop, with the truck bed swerving on the highway. Instead of calling out to the kids to wait and get back, he hurried them onto the bus, into what could have been a serious collision. It was not good judgment on his part, but the truck was able to stop and avoided a crash. The flag display was routine and seemed redundant; after all, the bus had flashing red lights. Today, most school buses have a stop sign that extends out from the side of the bus. Later on, a new bus route and new driver ended his term as flag boy.

CHAPTER 2
1953-1959

In 1953 the coronation of Elizabeth II took place; Edmund Hillary and Tensing Norgay were the first climbers to ascend Mount Everest; an armistice was signed ending hostilities in Korea; and Nikita Khrushchev was appointed general secretary of the Communist Party in the Soviet Union, which eventually led to what could be perceived as illogical cold war hysteria; the hydrogen bomb was under development in both the United States and the Soviet Union and in many schools the emotional reaction to the expansion of Cold War tactics contributed to action plans devised to protect the children. As Ron remembers it, his school conducted periodic rehearsals for a nuclear attack, ushering kids into a basement and a supposed shelter. Ron, along with his fellow students, enjoyed the departure from the usual classroom setting, unaware of the implication of the drills. He does not remember his early school years except to say he was a good student. He liked all his teachers but would have to refer to a yearbook to recognize them.

Some memories apart from school included trailing behind the explorations led by his sister: frightening their mother when she discovered them climbing to a top rafter window inside the barn above a cement floor; going through the back fields to the surprise of their grandparents at their home. His parents bought their first television in the early fifties. After school he and his sister watched Hopalong Cassidy Westerns, The Cisco Kid and Pancho, *The Howdy Doody Show*, *Andy's Gang* with Froggy the Gremlin, and *The Adventures of Superman*. Red Skelton and Milton Berle shows were popular family evening comedies, and on Sunday night *The Ed Sullivan Show* was a must-view. It is worth noting that while this was going on in his household, major events were taking place. In February 1954, Jonas Salk's polio vaccine was tested for the first time. In May, the Supreme Court's landmark unanimous decision, Brown v. Board of Education, ruled racial segregation violated the equal protection clause of the fourteenth amendment and was, therefore, unconstitutional. It must be mentioned that even though his passion for the Cleveland baseball team had not yet formed, its record of 111-43 is the best American League baseball win percentage (.721) of all time. However, their winning ways did not continue into the World Series; Cleveland lost to the New York Giants in four straight games.

As far as he can remember, the first movie he saw in a theater was *White Christmas*; the family went to the Bucyrus Schine Theatre to see the film. It left a lasting impression on him; the scenes of war, romance, comedy, and drama, interrupted by song and dance routines, were unforgettable. It may have been the only movie he saw in a theater prior to age sixteen.

Several times his family and the family of his mother's brother drove to East Harbor at Lake Erie in the summer for a day on the beach. Getting in the water one time, his feet lost contact with the sloping sand. Having never learned to swim, and with no one on shore in sight, his flailing struggles somehow got him back to a place of safety. After that experience, his fear of swimming or entering the water in a pool or on the beach lasted for years. Later, in college, he enrolled in a beginning swimming class but was not able to overcome his fear of getting in the water; he never learned to swim and received a generous grade of D for the course. Ten years after college he jumped into a swimming pool and taught himself how to dog paddle and float. He remembers it as a major accomplishment in his life.

In July 1955, Disneyland opened in Anaheim, California; the actor James Dean, age twenty-four, was killed in a car crash in

September; and in October *The Mickey Mouse Club* debuted on television and became a favorite show for him and his sister. In December, a more important incident occurred when African-Americans E.D. Nixon and Rosa Parks sparked a bus boycott in Montgomery, Alabama, the first large-scale protest against segregation in the United States.

The day before Ron's ninth birthday, Elvis Presley made his first television appearance when he performed on *The Dorsey Brothers Stage Show* in New York City. Two other performances that year on *The Milton Berle Show* and *The Ed Sullivan Show* garnered nationwide attention, and concurrent condemnation, because of Elvis's swiveling hips. Fidel Castro declared war on the Bautista regime in Cuba in April, eventually displacing him three years later. In November, President Eisenhower was reelected for a second four-year term after signing the Federal-Aid (Interstate) Highway Act in June. However, two other events of 1956 were memorable for Ron: planes colliding over the Grand Canyon and the Mau Mau uprising in Kenya, Africa.

During his grade school years, A grades kept him near the top of a class that fluctuated between twenty to twenty-five students in any one school year. He had an excellent memory and was a creative writer at an early age, but creativity was lacking when it came time for him to do an imaginative project for an upcoming PTA meeting at the beginning of the new school year. He does not remember how news of the plane collision came to his attention, especially at his young age; air travel would have been a fascinating achievement to him at the time. The thought of the passengers' emotions immediately after the collision, knowing they were probably doomed to die as the planes plummeted to the earth, bothered him. The crash so captured his thinking he decided to display newspaper articles and photos of the air disaster for the PTA project. It was not very inventive and was met with bewildered stares by the parents and teachers. Other students had developed brilliantly creative projects compared to his data gathering of a tragic event. As he remembers, the presentation did not affect his "top of the class" standing and his embarrassment lasted only a few days.

The Mau Mau uprising in Kenya did not involve a school project or dismay a PTA gathering, but he remembers it as a horrifying event because of a motion picture he watched at the time entitled *Safari*. Even while the rebellion was occurring the film was released in movie theatres and shown on television. It starred Victor Mature and Janet Leigh and depicted atrocities committed by the Mau Mau, including killing a little boy his age and the boy's mother. When he viewed the film as an adult, knowing the acts were staged, he was not at all affected. However, the real facts of the time show many people suffered as a result of the revolt; its leader was captured by the British Army in October 1956.

Ron would say the launch of Sputnik 1 by the Soviet Union in October 1957 did not detract from his enjoyment of the World Series that year between the New York Yankees and the (former) Milwaukee Braves; it may have been the first Series televised in rural Ohio. His mother had been a fan of players on the Cleveland team that won the World Series in 1948 and, probably trying to keep him from always being underfoot, encouraged him to watch the Series that year. Over the next few years, baseball became his passion, keeping score sheets of many Cleveland games while he listened on the radio. With no one to play with—his sister had different predispositions—he resorted to batting a ball around the barnyard in front of the barn, playing simulated games; different areas in the barnyard and on the barn represented the type of hit or out. If a gigantic hit placed the ball on the roof of the barn it was a home run. At the top of the high-peaked barn was a window—the same one his sister led him to at a younger age when they climbed on the rafters inside the barn. It never entered his mind he could hit a ball that high and hard, but one day, with utter disbelief and simultaneous dread, one of his hits shattered the glass. His father did not spank him often, but took him to the chicken yard next to the old outhouse and beat him with a stick when he learned Ron broke the window. His father had not been impressed with his ability to hit the ball so far.

The launch of Sputnik 2 in November got more of Ron's attention because the first animal, a dog named Laika, was aboard, and because teachers and other adults at school seemed to be worried about the increased power of the Soviet Union.

After his eleventh birthday, his father put him to work helping out on the farm. He taught him to drive a small Ford tractor and later to operate his four-ton flatbed truck in the back fields. His father's trust in his ability to do farm work and operate equipment increased his self-confidence. Because of his work on the farm, he selected agricultural and shop classes to take in junior high school, which automatically qualified him to be accepted into the Future Farmers of America; he agreed to join the FFA, but it was an expectation and not of much interest to him. He thought its motto "Learning to do, doing to learn, earning to live, living to serve," would have been better said "Learning to do, doing to earn, earning to live, living to serve," but he never suggested a change to anyone. FFA had requirements and goals for its members, but Ron was only interested in participating in its supervisory livestock projects. He enjoyed being around animals. His first project was caring for a Duroc hog—she had a litter of eight piglets. Later he raised two ewe lambs picked out of a flock of sheep his father purchased. If he ever thought of it, the idea of acquiring a trade skill like that of an electrician or plumber was ignored, nor was it ever suggested to him by his parents or teachers.

His father contributed labor and some capital working as a tenant farmer while the landlady provided the acreage and shared in the profits. The cattle, hogs, and chickens he raised gave their family an abundant supply of meat and eggs; vegetables from the garden complemented all the meals. His parents were a rung up from being dirt poor but always put plenty of food on the table. It was only later his mother began to complain of always having no money.

The farm fields were divided by a county road that intersected a state highway three miles south of Bucyrus. It was a half-mile drive east from the state highway to reach the western-most field of the undulating farm; beyond that field, a twenty-acre plot next to the road had a three-story house, barn, three wooden sheds to house machinery and grain, a hog house, and chicken coop. A detached garage west of the house was bordered on two sides by a lawn; an apple tree orchard was on the opposite side of the garage from the house. The small orchard had upwards of ten apple trees and two older apple trees were anchored in the lawn north of the garage. A very short driveway separated the house and garage and passed through a wooden gated fence that ran between the house and barnyard. Two large maple trees stood in front of the house along the road. East of the house was a plot of ground used as a vegetable garden. Later a round, wire corn crib was put up next to the barn. The gently rolling landscape of the remaining acreage consisted of ten fields of various size, each enclosed by wire fencing.

The Ford tractor his father taught him to drive was a small, twenty-five horsepower 1947 model 2N. Ron looked forward to the instruction apprehensively. As he remembers it, the first time he was put in the driver's seat his leg had to be fully extended in order for his foot to depress the clutch; the transmission was engaged in the slowest gear. His father cautioned him to release the clutch gradually and then positioned himself directly in front of the tractor, probably with the idea of conducting a slow, forward movement. However, while trying to follow his directions, Ron's foot slipped off the clutch, causing the tractor to jerk forward and his father to jump quickly to one side to avoid being run over. Ron immediately obeyed his father's "depress the clutch again" command and stopped the tractor. To his surprise, the expected tongue lashing never came; his father was patient and told him to try again. Soon, he conquered the procedure and fear of the tractor and his father went on instructing him as he drove around the field; later on, his training extended to driving a larger Farmall tricycle-style tractor, pulling behind it harrowing equipment, discs, and eventually a plow. It was a few years later that his father taught him to operate the flatbed truck.

Ron's apprehension seated on the tractor was in direct contrast to his confidence when he was in the kitchen with his mother while she prepared her usual sumptuous dinner. She liked to cook and her plump body testified to how much she appreciated her own meals. Later in life, he discovered photos of her svelte form as a young woman and understood another reason his father may have been attracted to her besides any culinary skills. The kitchen was roomy with a center table and chairs, an old icebox, a refrigerator, electric oven, and an abundance of counter space alongside a sink positioned under a window that looked out onto a side yard and the garage. The icebox and large walk-in pantry provided storage space and another room off the kitchen housed an old-style wringer washing machine. Clothes were hung out to dry on a wooden rack in cold weather, but during the warm months his mother hung the clothes on a line outside.

The kitchen could be entered from the barnyard through a passage gate on a footpath of cement slabs separating a small grass lawn; the slabs ran from the fence to three semi-circular concrete steps under a covering porch roof to a back door. A short hall off the kitchen passed a half-bath to a stairway—also accessed by a second back door—descending to a roomy cellar dominated by a large coal furnace and several rooms for coal storage and one used primarily for canned goods. From the kitchen, a passage doorway opened into the dining room where a side door closest to the garage was the main entrance to the home. The rest of the downstairs rooms included a living room, front room and parlor. Two sets of stairs, one from the dining room and one from near a seldom-used front porch entrance—from a seldom-used front porch—led up to four bedrooms and a bathroom on the second floor. Ron's sister shared a bedroom with him until she advocated for one of her own. He claimed an aptitude for interior decorating that helped him convert a small unused room next to his bedroom into a playroom complete with desk, chairs and storage shelves for board games. A roomy upper attic was accessed by another flight of stairs, but Ron never realized it could have been converted into another storage or playroom.

Dueling rocket launches by the United States and the Soviet Union were dominating the rest of the news at the end of the decade along with the creation of NASA and the granting of statehood to Alaska and Hawaii. Advancing to junior high school during those years did not affect Ron's studies or class standing. Inheriting some of his mother's musical talent may have led him to be chosen to perform as actor/singer in two musical productions: as emcee in a "This Is Your Life" show singing "The Yellow Rose of Texas" and as the interlocutor in a minstrel show. After those performances, one teacher suggested she might be able to get him on the radio, but her efforts, if made, were not successful.

His parents went on outings periodically, driving around the county and to places of interest. Knowing his passion for baseball, especially Cleveland Indians baseball, they went to Cleveland in the summer of 1959 a couple of times to attend a baseball game. He got the feeling his parents enjoyed them as much as he did. It was a fun time for the whole family. He recalled the thrilling experience of entering the ballpark for the first time at the age of twelve: the hustle and bustle of all the people on the walkways underneath the stands of the enormous, old Municipal Stadium was palpable; vendors were selling souvenirs and food everywhere he looked. Then a walk up a ramp to view the playing area and its huge expanse of lush, immaculately tended green grass took his breath away. The impeccably prepared dirt infield with the bright white bases and home plate contrasted nicely with the grass too. He was able to recall, to some extent, that same feeling whenever he returned to a stadium to attend a game. The whole family went to another game that year, memorable because Ted Williams of the Boston Red Sox hit a home run deep into a section of the right field stands that extended only a short distance into fair territory beyond the playing area. Williams, though not on the Cleveland team, had become his favorite baseball player. He and his parents were seated in the upper deck on the left side of home plate and their view of the ball sailing high and deep into the stands was unobstructed. During future ballpark visits Ron saw Willie Mays, Hank Aaron, and Frank Robinson, among others, play ball in Cincinnati's Crosley Field before the Cincinnati team moved to its new stadium years later.

CHAPTER 3
1960-1967

The decade of the sixties had a normal enough beginning for Ron. His schoolwork continued routinely, but most of his memories relate to summertime activities on the farm; he helped his father in the fields or got in the way of his mother in the house. He recalled one summer day she went to Bucyrus to do grocery shopping and took him and his sister with her. When they returned home, the two large apple trees in the yard next to the apple orchard had been toppled by what must have been a huge wind. The house and other buildings were not affected; apparently a brief isolated storm had blown over the trees. Whatever happened, his mother was relieved not to have been home at the time. The growing civil rights movement in the South never caught his attention and his parents did not talk about it, although they probably heard the news of more sit-ins at diners by African-Americans demanding expanded freedom and liberties.

In North Carolina and Nashville in early 1960, African-Americans were protesting segregation. It was not an issue in northern rural Ohio, but spying and spy planes interested Ron. The news that the Soviet Union shot down an American U2 spy plane caused Cold War tensions to continue to mount; it became a diplomatic crisis of a high order. Later that year, the presidential election caught his attention for the first time because of the debates between Vice President Richard Nixon and Senator John Kennedy. Of course, Kennedy won the closest election of the twentieth century, but many who listened on radio thought Nixon would win. Kennedy's cool demeanor during the first-ever televised debates, compared to Nixon's chalky appearance, might have made the difference in the final outcome.

Soon after Ron's fourteenth birthday, his father taught him to drive his two-and-one-half-ton flatbed truck. His father used the truck at home but bought it to haul grain, fertilizer, and other bagged feeds working part-time at the Bucyrus Farm Bureau. After one long day harvesting corn he instructed Ron to follow him in the truck filled with corn while he drove the tractor and corn harvester to the farmyard from the back field. Trying to steer the truck from the field into a dirt lane, Ron panicked and continued to step on the accelerator causing the truck to break through the wire fence bordering another field until it stopped against a fence post. Ron's expectation was, at best, a tongue lashing. But ever the patient teacher, his father backed the truck out of the fence and sat beside Ron as he drove the truck the remaining distance to the road at which point his father took over and continued the short drive to the farm yard. He repaired the hole in the fence later.

Nineteen sixty-one was an eventful year around the world. President Kennedy established the Peace Corps effective March 1. The Bay of Pigs assault on Cuba failed in April, causing more Cold War posturing between the United States and the Soviet Union, especially after Yuri Gagarin, a Soviet pilot, became the first man in space. In May, less than one month after Gagarin's flight, the first American in space, Alan Shepherd, commanded a Mercury capsule suborbital flight. President Kennedy then announced the start of the Apollo program and its goal of landing a man on the moon by the end of the decade. In October, *The Dick Van Dyke Show* premiered on television about the same time Ron's parents were making final arrangements to buy their own farm. In December, a public auction of farm equipment and household items preceded the move to their new home, causing anxious anticipation for Ron and his sister and, no doubt, for his parents too.

After renting a farm for fourteen years, his parents were able, somehow, to afford the down payment on a 160-acre farm near Nevada, Ohio, in neighboring Wyandot County, about ten miles west of the farm they had rented in Crawford County. The family moved there in the winter of 1962, just about the time of Ron's fifteenth birthday. One piece of equipment not sold was an old Allis Chalmers tractor his father bought and restored and used occasionally; a crank at the front of the tractor had to be turned to engage the starter. When his father wanted Ron to use the tractor, he started it because it was too difficult for Ron to turn the crank. His father wanted him to drive it to their new home on the county roads and told him how to get there; it was Ron's first time driving a long distance on roadways. He remembers being afraid he would stall the tractor at a crossroad and not be able to restart it with the crank; he approached all the intersections with caution but never had any problems. It turned out to be a fun ride.

1938 Allis Chalmers tractor

The new home was located on a township highway one--quarter mile west of the county line separating Wyandot and Crawford counties and, consequently, in a different school district, three-quarters of a mile east of a state route that continued north from the county road intersection two miles to the village of Nevada. The house was smaller than the previous home; it was two stories with a bathroom and five small rooms downstairs, including the kitchen, and four small upstairs bedrooms. One downstairs washroom contained the first electric washing and dryer machines purchased for his mother to use, replacing the old wringer washing machine and dryer rack she used in their rented home. A wide, roofed front porch extended the length of the house; the porch had two doors, each door entering into a different front room, but seldom used for visitors. A shed-like building was connected to the back of the house by a small mudroom; the mudroom had five passage doors: a side entrance door; a back exit; a door to the shed; a cellar door; and a kitchen door into the house. The side entrance door into the house kitchen was the main entrance, even for visitors. The shed was remodeled a few years later by his parents into a comfortable summer house; they installed a wood burning stove near one end surrounded by linoleum. Most of the rest of the room was carpeted.

Ron helped his father install a wide brick-paved patio at the rear of the house years later that extended to the length of the shed; the patio butted up to the back exit door. A garage was several steps from another summer house entrance and a large red barn and a large wooden shed were in the farmyard separated by a white picket fence. A large yard circled three sides of the house, the back of which ended at a large garden area. A stone lane ran from the road along the other side of the house. Across the lane in front of the barn was another large yard bordered on the lane and road by eight maple trees. The property had an eighty-acre woods; a running brook divided lower and higher elevations; a long straight grass lane ran from the farmyard between two fields. The lane turned right at the end of the fields away from a small wooded meadow, crossed a winding creek below a tree-studded hillside and ended in wooded acreage. The landscape was completely different from the previous farm that had gently rolling tillable acres unadorned by wood or water habitat. Instead of ten fields on the rented farm, the new acreage had four fenced fields.

Ron's sister was halfway through her senior year in high school and wanted to complete her school year with familiar classmates so they decided to walk the quarter mile, oftentimes through snow and rain, to meet the bus at the county line road. With only another year before several schools consolidated, Ron decided to continue to walk and meet the bus the next school year; staying in a familiar setting and with established classmate friends appealed to him too. His father had already decided to work full-time at the Farm Bureau in Bucyrus before the move to their new home but brought a few cattle and sheep with him from the old farm. Ron continued to care for two ewe lambs; he sold his Duroc sow. His new FFA project was a Berkshire hog. Trying to care for the hog was a waste of time. She smothered half a litter of her piglets, laying on them soon after giving birth to them; his father sold her to another farmer, ending Ron's hog venture. He should have realized caring for hogs was not in his DNA. He fainted while castrating the Duroc piglets at their former farm, much to the astonishment of his agriculture teacher. The procedure and odor of the antibiotics were too much for him. However, he enjoyed caring for the lambs; he named them Lamb Chop and Wooly.

He remembers Lamb Chop being very cooperative when he took her to the county fair. She was awarded a second-place red ribbon; at the last minute the sheep judge moved her from a blue first-place ribbon line. What had not been explained to him was lambs shown at the fair were usually sold to be butchered. He refused to sell Lamb Chop; she came home with him and lived a long, but unproductive, life. She and Wooly had little success birthing and caring for their lambs, but always seemed to have an "I'm better than you" attitude among the other sheep; it was as if they knew they were special, standing tall with heads held high whenever Ron approached the flock while the rest of the sheep foraged.

His parents began attending the Lutheran church in Nevada. Both he and his sister were baptized at the church, but he had already been baptized at the age of five in a ceremony at a Church of Christ in the village of Kirkpatrick, near their former home. He didn't understand the meaning of baptism or why he needed to be rebaptized; it was never made clear to him. He thought the second ceremony may have been because his sister had never been baptized and the church pastor thought she would be more comfortable going through the ceremony with him. But he remembers the pastor encouraging his parents to also have him baptized a Lutheran. Whatever the reason, Ron didn't realize at the time that the act of baptism symbolized the inward phenomenon of coming to and accepting Jesus Christ as real; that it was a means by which those who believe in Christ can be forever reconciled to God.

The New Testament Gospels of Matthew, Mark, and Luke tell the story of John baptizing Jesus with water prior to beginning his ministry, and Lutherans believe baptism is symbolic of God's love for all; they are liberated from sin and death by being joined to the death and resurrection of Jesus through water combined with the promises of his words in the gospels. Ron was mostly ignorant of this belief. His parents had instructed him well in the idea of right and wrong but not sin. To be liberated from death sounded good but how exactly did that work? In any case, going through the ceremony again was an uncomfortable experience, as was attending church—the services always seemed so joyless. After the second baptism, his attitude was "Whew, I got that out of the way." But what he didn't know was baptism is not intended to be a "one and done" event but the first milestone in a lifelong journey of faith, in a community of other believers in the world, to those called to work and serve by the grace of God and faith through prayer and service, and to "proclaim the mystery of Christ" (Colossians 4:3); a mysterious path for those who do not believe in Christ and one Ron did not follow for a long time.

Ron was shy around the girls at school and did not interact with them except in class. He never seemed to be relaxed in their company even though his mother had been a great caregiver and comforter in his youth and his sister was a guiding force and playmate when he was very young. He reasoned that because of puberty and relationships with the other boys his attitude toward girls began to change; he began to look at the opposite sex as an object, not trying to understand their feelings or personhood. He had a fantasy crush on Annette Funicello, who appeared on television's *The Mickey Mouse Club* a few years earlier. His infatuation shifted to an attractive new girl at school even though she became involved in a relationship with a basketball player two years her senior. But then a cute girl caught his eye one day at church. Working up enough courage to ask her out was not practical because he had not turned sixteen and had no driver's license, but a school classmate who knew he liked her suggested they go on a double date. Being a year older than Ron, the classmate already had his driver's license and his parents let him drive their car. It was a humiliating experience. After mustering up the courage to ask her out, his classmate turned up without a date and "chaperoned" the evening, watching them in his rearview mirror and later castigating him for not "making a move.". It was his only date during his high school years, and he eventually resorted to self-gratification to satisfy his sexual desires.

With the move to their new home, other events that same year did not go unnoticed. John Glenn, an Ohio native, was the first American to orbit the Earth in space followed a few months later by Scott Carpenter; the flights caught the attention of most everyone. So did the Cuban missile crisis that dominated the airwaves during September and October. One event that went under the radar was Operation Chopper, the first use of United States helicopters in Vietnam. On a lighter note, Johnny Carson began his thirty-year run hosting *The Tonight Show*. More significant to Ron, and before the above events occurred, Ginger died soon after their move. She had survived and flourished many years on the farm and was a cherished family member. She helped his father when he herded cattle, hogs, and sheep from one farm lot to another. Her ears were pushed back by the wind with her head out a moving car window or as she stood stiff legged on bouncing hay wagons; she fought groundhogs, raccoon, possum, and other critters as big in stature as her small frame to near exhaustion. But in her old age, the move to a new home seemed to be too much for her frail body. The severe winter that year did not help. One morning Ron found her dead body in the barn. She lay stiff from the cold on a bed of straw he had prepared for her. Pleading with his mother to let her come in the warm house had been to no avail. She adamantly refused to let an animal, even their beloved dog, inside. To make things worse, the bones were ravished by scavengers after he tried to bury her in the frozen ground.

All the talk at the end of the 1963 school year was about the impending consolidation of four county schools. Students numbering less than twenty in the school Ron attended would join students from three other similarly sized schools to make a total of eighty-six pupils who would comprise the first graduating class of Wynford, a new rural school less than two miles west of Bucyrus. Anticipating that merger overshadowed his growing dissatisfaction with farm work that had occupied most of his prior summer days. Becoming involved with the Boy Scouts or other similar activities had never been discussed with him as an option, maybe because those programs were not available in the area. But being a baseball fanatic, his parents let him join a summer baseball Pony League. The patron of the team picked him to be player/manager after watching him during tryouts; he knew his playing talents were limited. He took the job as manager to heart and believed his managerial skills were more than adequate.

Ron proudly referred to a memorable decision he made in the league championship game. His team's best pitcher, usually in control every time he pitched, had been struggling the whole game; when Ron's team scored in the top of an inning, his pitcher failed to hold the lead. The seven-inning game went back and forth like that until the last inning. Ron's team had gone ahead by one run in the top of the seventh but the opposing team loaded the bases in the bottom of the inning with no outs. Whoever won the game would be the champion. Should he leave his struggling starter in the game and hope for the best or make a change? He opted for a change. Nick, a scatter-armed left-handed pitcher and sometime position player, was stationed in left field. Ron liked Nick. He had a strikeout pitch if he could control it, but he could also be notably wild. When he called him in to relieve their star pitcher, he heard some players in his dugout moaning with apprehension. But Nick struck out the next three batters, preserving the win and securing the championship for the team; Nick was the hero of the day. After that summer, Nick and the other players never crossed his path again.

One other memory from that summer was a trip to a drive-in movie with three of his male classmates. They enjoyed watching two films that were destined to begin a new movie phenomenon: Sean Connery starred as James Bond in the films *Dr. No* and *From Russia with Love*. His enthusiasm for Cleveland baseball carried over to the pro football Cleveland Browns during the era Jim Brown was their star running back. The only pro football game he ever attended was with his father and his Farm Bureau co-workers at Cleveland in September 1963. Jim Brown had a great day against the Washington Redskins, rushing for a total of 162 yards, including eighty-yard and ten-yard touchdowns; he caught three passes for 100 yards including an eighty-three-yard touchdown catch and run. The Browns won their last championship in 1964 before the origination of the Super Bowl. After their subsequent move to Baltimore in 1995, his interest in pro football, and football in general, waned.

Less than three months later, a new school friend from Nevada he met earlier in the summer, also named Ron, prodded him to skip class and roam the halls of Wynford High. They were having a great time until another student approached them with the shocking news President Kennedy had been assassinated. The school was dismissed and everyone returned to their homes; it was a sobering event. Vice President Lyndon Johnson was sworn in as president aboard Air Force One the same day. Incredibly, two days later as Ron watched a live television broadcast, Jack Ruby penetrated a crowd of onlookers in the basement of a Dallas, Texas, police station, shooting and killing Lee Harvey Oswald, the suspected assassin.

Wynford completed its first high school year in the spring of 1964 and Ron was counted among the graduating students. Attending a new school had been a challenge for him. His standing as the top male pupil in his small former school was no longer significant among the dozens of new classmates. His grades, along with his status and self-confidence, plummeted. He could not remember trying to attract a girlfriend; his efforts were constantly thwarted by fear and confusion with regard to intimacy and a lack of financial resources. Retaining a measure of self-worth allowed him to make a few new male friends. Don became a lifelong friend but Ron, with whom he had roamed the Wynford halls, was killed in the Vietnam War. During a visit to the Vietnam War Memorial in Washington, DC, a few years later, his tears were genuine after finding Ron's name inscribed on its marble wall.

Graduating from high school without a plan for the future and no general aim or purpose led to his decision to go to college. He was no longer interested in farming and had no other goal in mind except for a possible career as a sportscaster, but not just any sportscaster. His specific objective was to announce Cleveland Indians games. He had listened to Jimmy Dudley announce Cleveland baseball on the radio for years and was convinced it would be a grand way to make a living. It was a very indefinite occupational goal. On the other hand, going to college was a way to avoid being drafted by the army. By then the Vietnam War had escalated but his understanding of those events could best be called uninformed, at least until his friend's death two years later. War or no war, the army was not for him. Joining the army seemed to Ron to be a daunting choice so, as he had done when he joined the FFA, he chose a more satisfactory path and was accepted to attend Kent State University, applying to that institution because it had a low tuition rate—$350 per year—and was close to home. The summer before beginning college he noticed the tax return paperwork of his father. His meager adjusted gross income was probably lower than the medium family income at the time; taxes and other deductions would have produced a significantly lower net income that included all his farm and employment earnings and wages. During all his formative and teen years the family never lacked food, clothing or other necessities. The ability of his father to care for the family on limited income did not impress him until later.

The summer before college his father paid full-scale wages to Ron to help him on his job at the Farm Bureau. The earnings paid for most of his first-year tuition. However, his mother had begun constantly berating his father about their money situation. One day Ron sat down for lunch with his parents. His sister was not at home, having enrolled in a school of cosmetology in Columbus. His mother erupted with a stream of criticism directed at his father; her continual hounding caused Ron to intercede in his defense. At the same time his father began to sob uncontrollably and pleaded for his mother to stop her verbal attacks. Ron couldn't believe what was taking place; an indelible impression of his mother's chiding that day stayed with him for a long time. He eventually forgot and forgave her outburst and sensed her attitude began to change after the incident. She gradually settled into a more supportive role. As far as he knew, the only other time his father cried was after she died in an automobile accident. Ron said his use of alcohol began about this time, not to say it was encouraged by what had happened at home. His mother's father had given him a first taste of beer. Since the legal drinking age in Ohio at the time was eighteen, his older classmate friends happily supplied him with alcoholic beverages until his birthday the following year.

Looking from a different perspective, 1964 produced some lighter, if not electrifying, moments. The Beatles made their first appearances in the United States, in March the game show *Jeopardy* premiered, the Ford Mustang rolled off the production line for the first time, and the Browns defeated the Baltimore Colts 27-0 in the NFL championship game. Probably the most significant event, however, was the passage of the Civil Rights Act that outlawed discrimination on the basis of race, color, sex, religion, and national origin, later to include sexual orientation and gender identity. President Johnson, who signed the act into law, was elected to serve a full term in November.

At Kent, reading and studying literature became one of his favorite pastimes. In his youth, classics such as Daniel Defoe's tale of Robinson Crusoe and the stories of James Fenimore Cooper grabbed his attention. In college he read literature by Fitzgerald, Melville, and Steinbeck in his spare time. Hemingway's *The Sun Also Rises* was one of his favorites. As he got older, literature similar to Arthur Conan Doyle's *The Complete Works of Sherlock Holmes* piqued his interest. Conrad Richter's trilogy *The Awakening Land: The Trees, The Fields, The Town* and short stories by O. Henry and Somerset Maugham were enjoyable to read. He tried to avoid attaching too much symbolism to an author's work, instead enjoying it on its own merits, describing himself as a literalist without dismissing symbolism as a literary element. Later in life he discovered many passages in the Bible were presented symbolically—Jesus as the sacrificial lamb; the rock as the strength and security God provides his people. He also came to be interested in and understand the well-known idea of Jonah being a type of Christ. Jesus said, "A wicked and adulterous generation looks for a miraculous sign, but none will be given it except the sign of Jonah" (Mat. 16:4). The whale swallowing Jonah and then regurgitating him after three days symbolized the death, burial, and resurrection of Jesus.

His friend Don decided to attend Kent too; they roomed together in Clark Hall their first year and, as he recalled, it nearly ended their friendship. Other people around the world were taking notice of hot spots. In February the United States sent its first combat troops to Vietnam and followed the next month with the first sustained bombing campaign of the newly declared war. Events at home were in turmoil too. Unbeknownst to him, a civil rights march in 1965, led by Martin Luther King Jr., from Selma to Montgomery, Alabama, succeeded after several thousand activists had previously joined in a march that came to be known as Bloody Sunday. Having lived in nonblack communities all his life, the civil rights movement didn't stir up any emotions in him. African-American enrollment at Kent State was less than 5% of the student population and the movement did not seem relevant to him. Sad to say, his passion was limited to a field of baseball dreams and not on a dream of unity as expressed by Dr. King.

When the Astrodome opened in Houston for the 1965 Major League baseball season it seemed inconceivable to Ron a baseball game could be played indoors; a stadium would have to be large enough to confine the flight of a baseball, plus the sport seemed more suited for outdoor play. His favorite player for Cleveland in the early sixties was third baseman Max Alvis. That summer he drove his parents to Cleveland to see a weekend doubleheader against the Minnesota Twins. They watched a Cleveland three-run rally in the bottom of the ninth of the first game fall a run short to the Twins. Max Alvis had two hits in the game but struck out at a key moment during the ninth inning. The second game appeared to be going the same way. Fan favorite Rocky Colavito had hit a home run but the Twins were leading by two runs. His parents wanted to leave before the game ended but agreed to stay until the bitter end. Max Alvis had not been in the lineup for the Indians in the second game, but with two out and a man on base in the bottom of the ninth inning he was called on to pinch-hit. As Ron hoped for the improbable, Max Alvis drove a home run deep into the left field seats. Sitting in the upper deck down the left field line, Ron said he watched the ball sail past their view as if it was moving in slow motion; the ball was not rotating but seemed to push through the air on a steady, straight path. His hero had come through with a game-tying home run, and Cleveland went on to win the game in eleven innings and is one of his favorite memories.

His main social contacts during the second and third years at Kent were new roommates joining him in a McDowell Hall suite, one a Jewish man from Pittsburgh and two men from near Lorain, Ohio. In their third year together, one of his roommates from Lorain asked him to sing at his wedding; he also later formed a band and asked him to be the singer. His Jewish roommate invited Ron to his wedding too; he followed the tradition of breaking the glass at the conclusion of the ceremony. They all were aware of the escalating space race. The Soviet Union launched several probes to the moon; the unmanned Luna 9 was the first controlled landing; Luna 10 followed and was the first successful orbiting probe. Meanwhile, NASA continued its Gemini program that performed the first docking of spacecraft in Earth orbit; Neil Armstrong and David Scott were command pilot and pilot of the first successful docking mission. The Supreme Court case Miranda v. Arizona was decided in June 1966. It ordered the police to administer to suspects their rights before questioning them. The *Star Trek* series premiered in September but Ron and his roommates devoted most of their spare time to playing cards; euchre was the game of choice.

Ron had no female relationships at Kent. His only blind date turned out to be with an unattractive girl. From their suite, women in rooms adjacent to their dormitory could be seen if their curtains were open. After watching women in one particular room over a period of time, one of his roommates obtained their telephone number. Suspecting the curtain was left open on purpose, Ron was asked to be the guinea pig and call their room to make a date with one of them. His call was met by an appealing voice; she agreed to accompany him to a campus football game sight unseen. Ron was embarrassed when they met. She approached him wearing an unappealing outfit and had coke bottle glasses and stringy hair. He took her to the game but at halftime it began to rain; it was a good excuse to end the date early. Although their dormitories shared a common dining hall, he never saw her again. In retrospect, he wondered if she disguised herself to look bad as a prank. His roommates got a big laugh out of it. They generally always had a good time together but did not stay in touch after graduating from Kent.

Ron not only worked for his father at the Farm Bureau the summer before college but also the following summer. Those earnings, and money earned during the next two summers working at the Ohio Locomotive Crane Company in Bucyrus, paid for his tuition and room and board. During his first year at Kent a position in the dining hall kitchen offered a few extra dollars but his long-held desire to be a sportscaster—specifically to broadcast Cleveland Indian baseball games—led him to get a nonpaid position one night each week on the local FM radio station. A script called for him to recite the classical music being played that night, but after watching the engineers do all the work for the show, he became disillusioned. At the same time, he accepted the futility of such a narrowly defined goal as sportscaster for a specific team; any thoughts of having a career in that field had become apparent and were unrealistic. Many teams had already begun to hire ex-players to broadcast their games. Herb Score, a former Cleveland pitcher, had begun announcing Cleveland games several years earlier. It was obvious persons with expertise or special connections were the ones being considered to broadcast baseball games.

At Kent, students were encouraged to decide on a major field of study leading to graduation by their third year. With his thoughts of sportscasting derailed, Ron decided upon a Bachelor of Science in business administration with an accounting major. Accounting was known to be a fine, prosperous occupation and the possibility of earning "big bucks" was an attractive incentive. Money, or the lack thereof, being such a factor in his life it seemed like a reasonable goal. But, like his previous high school experience with the Future Farmers of America, a degree in accounting to fulfill a college requirement was an expectation and not of great interest to him. He enjoyed studying the accounting basics but was not motivated to analyze its practices and procedures although his effort to be successful drove him to study with due diligence.

Many stories highlighted the news in 1967. The first Super Bowl was played in January. Later that month, three astronauts died when their Apollo 1 space capsule caught fire on the ground at the Kennedy Space Center. In April the first man to die on a space mission was a Soviet Union cosmonaut; the parachute to slow his reentry to Earth failed to open. But much closer to home, an unexpected diagnosis of schizophrenia and subsequent hospitalization of his sister effectively ended her work and social life. She had completed cosmetology training and was working as a hairstylist in a Bucyrus salon, driving to and from work using her parent's car until she could earn enough money to get one of her own. She was very pretty but, like Ron, shy around other people; a man so enamored by her attractiveness followed her home from work one evening. They began dating until the onset of her illness. Ron's parents concealed her condition from Ron at first, suspecting her condition might affect his school work. She was hospitalized for about a year before his parents brought her home where she lived for the next twenty years. Knowing his sister had a mental illness obviously distressed his parents; not until years later were they able to accept that her illness was a genetic condition and was not caused by her environment during childhood and teen years. It disturbed Ron when he heard of his sister's illness. Regrettably, her condition and his general lack of motivation provided a good excuse for him not to finish his course requirements. Rather than drop out of college, all his assigned program courses for spring quarter were marked incomplete at his request.

In June, Israel won a six-day war with its Arab neighbors. Ten justices had been confirmed to the Supreme Court during Ron's lifetime, but in October Thurgood Marshall became the first African-American judge appointed to the high court after being nominated by President Johnson and confirmed by the Senate. Later that same year Carl Stokes became one of the first African-American mayors to take office in the United States after an election in Cleveland. Ron began his fourth year that autumn at Kent in an off-campus house with a new housemate, a teaching assistant in mathematics. They began drinking together a lot on weekends. Ron never had a great supply of money to spend. He received five dollars for incidentals from his parents two or three times a month but his father often complained about sending him money. Somehow Ron made it stretch to allow for his new weekend habit.

At the end of the fall quarter an internship with an accounting firm was offered to accounting majors as an option for winter quarter to take the place of classroom work. The offer included internship programs with several Ohio firms and one in New York City. S.D. Leidesdorf & Co., known as a small firm in New York City, accepted Ron's application; their main attribute touted to prospective clients at the time was, unlike most accounting firms, they had never been sued. Ultimately, they grew into the largest accounting firm in the city, continuing to be known for their lofty standards before merging with another public accounting firm years later. Ron remembered going to work in New York as a scary, exciting adventure; Ohio would no longer be his home, at least for the next three months. In early December his first jet airplane flight took him from Columbus to New York and an eventual room in a west side 63rd Street YMCA between Central Park and Columbus Circle in Manhattan. The room became his residence during the winter of 1967/68.

S.D. Leidesdorf made arrangements for the temporary YMCA room, offering to find him an apartment once he arrived in the city, but with no extra finances the YMCA seemed tolerable enough for three months. From 63rd Street, he took the subway to the huge Grand Central Station followed by a short walk to their office; he no longer recalls its location but thinks it was on Madison Avenue. At their headquarters a two-week training session began his paid internship after which the firm gave him two auditing assignments: the first was six weeks at Bali Bra in Bayonne, New Jersey; a second six-week job was at the Maidenform Garment store on Thirty-Second Street in Manhattan. The unofficial title given to him by a co-worker after the second undergarment assignment was "bra man." The subway was his mode of transportation and helped familiarize him with the surroundings. To get to Bayonne he rode the subway to the Madison Square Garden exit that connected to the Port Authority Bus Terminal. From there a bus transported him through the Holland Tunnel to Jersey City, New Jersey; a local bus got him to Bayonne. At the end of the day another local bus took him to a George Washington Bridge bus stop unless a co-worker gave him a ride. Across the bridge by bus and a short walk to a 179th Street subway station returned him to the YMCA. It was a grueling dawn to dusk schedule. However, getting to Maidenform was an easy B train subway commute from Columbus Circle to Herald Square's Thirty-Fourth Street exit and a two-block walk to the garment store.

    A friend from Kent invited him to spend Christmas and the New Year holiday with him at his parents' home in Queens. They were very welcoming and Ron enjoyed the holidays with them but it was uncomfortable to be in a strange household. His friend's father had an imposing, exhausting work ethic, laboring at two full-time jobs back-to-back in Manhattan. After the holidays Ron accompanied him on the Long Island railroad commute back to the city. His friend returned to Kent and they never met again. Ron's financial situation and work schedule, general lack of initiative, and the usual fear and confusion concerning intimacy with the opposite sex kept him from even seeking someone to date. Mickey, a fellow YMCA roomer, attached himself to a reluctant Ron and sought his companionship. Mickey was very much like the Ratso character played by Dustin Hoffman in the movie *Midnight Cowboy*, fascinating and disgusting at the same time. Ron tried to avoid him but they visited several places together: concourse level dining in Rockefeller Center, Radio City Music Hall, and Chinatown. Several friends from Ohio visited Ron at different times, always making it to the top of the Empire State Building at some point during their visit. When a McDowell Hall roommate came to see him, they stopped at Jilly's, a restaurant/bar known to be frequented by Frank

Sinatra. He wasn't there but Steve Lawrence, Edie Gormet, Robert Goulet and his wife at the time, Carol Lawrence, were seated close to their table. Earlier that night Steve and Edie had performed in the Broadway musical production of *Golden Rainbow*. Ron enjoyed the show, especially the acting of Steve Lawrence, but it was refuted by the critics and lasted only several weeks in the theater. He went to see two other shows: *Mame*, starring Angela Lansbury, and *The Prime of Miss Jean Brodie* with Zoe Caldwell in the title role, but has no lasting impression of their performances or the shows.

At the end of his internship S.D. Leidesdorf offered him a position with their firm contingent on his graduation from Kent State. But the time Ron spent with them convinced him accounting was not a good career choice; he believed the work of an auditor would be boring and repetitive and not something he would enjoy. As it turned out, many of his future jobs were accounting-related but did not offer nearly the financial rewards a position with S.D. Leidesdorf & Co. would have provided. As expected, his decision did not sit well with his parents. His father, especially, wondered if his studies were just a waste of time; should he have used the time to learn a skill and in that way be a productive citizen? His reasons for attending college were definitely open to question and in Ron's mind his father may have been right. As it turned out, he finished his studies and got his degree with a major in accounting, which proved helpful in the long run.

CHAPTER 4
1968-1973

In many ways the first half of 1968 was characterized by despair, even though in January the live recording "At Folsom Prison" revitalized the career of Johnny Cash. But the continued escalation of the Vietnam war punctuated by the My Lai Massacre atrocity along with the assassinations of Martin Luther King Jr. and Robert Kennedy left people wondering about the state of the union. However, following those events Ron signed up for a summer work/study program in England with Russ, a friend he met through Don. They traveled to London with a group of about thirty students, most of whom went on to work at various locations throughout Europe. A two-day sightseeing tour in London preceded the various assignments. He and Russ were scheduled to work at Butlin's Holiday Camp at Clacton-on-Sea on England's east coast. The camp could be considered a working-class version of Disneyland; visitors could stay at the camp for an extended time if they chose. Although Clacton-on-Sea resort is now closed, three of the ten original seaside resorts remain open, incorporated under a new name.

Russ's work assignment was cleaning and caring for the outdoor swimming pool. Ron's job was operating the sole escalator, reversing the up and down movement of the stairs so visitors could move to and from a second-floor dining hall. A few of the visitors had never seen an escalator and several were nervous about riding on it. One older, tall, and solidly built woman from Wales had to be convinced it was safe. When she stepped on the stairs her feet moved upward on the stair but the rest of her body tilted backward to a final prone position. It reminded Ron of a timber tree slowly falling backward. He called out to another diner to hit the escalator stop button while supporting the woman's body as best he could; other diners helped him lift her to an upright position. She probably never tried to use the moving stairs again. Although unnerving at the time, in retrospect it is a humorous memory of his time at the camp. Ron connected briefly with two women, one from Czechoslovakia and one from France, but a more serious relationship with either woman was short-circuited by his same old problems, fear of intimacy and lack of financial resources.

All in all it was a relaxing time in England; little work and no study. Students from all over Europe worked there and a lot of the discussions involved Vietnam and the violence taking place in America. During their time at the camp, riots and protests preceding the Democratic National Convention in Chicago caused even more talk about what was going on in the United States. Russ developed a relationship with another camp employee, an English woman from Leicester. The three of them spent a good amount of time together, even visiting her home town, but his only memory of being in Leicester is of a dance hall they went to one night. An image of her parent's home is also unclear. One weekend Russ went to Cambridge. Ron also traveled to the university at a later date but his memory of the day he was there is vague. At the end of summer, they rejoined the rest of the student group in Brussels after crossing the English Channel by ferry boat and then going on by train; the whole group then returned to the United States.

A favorite part of the return trip for Russ, but something Ron cannot remember, was a hydrofoil excursion to the Isle of Wight. However, Ron thoroughly enjoyed their stay at a bed and breakfast at an inconspicuous three-story brownstone walk-up in a row of houses in Dover before embarking on their channel crossing. The woman owner served them morning wake-up coffee in their third story bedroom and a hearty breakfast in the basement dining room after they got dressed. In Brussels, they visited a night club with two women students in their group, Ron asked one woman to dance to several Frank Sinatra songs he asked the DJ to play. They twirled around the polished floor wonderfully together, in his opinion; the best dance routines he can ever remember performing. Unfortunately, his memory of the girl is not clear at all.

When he and Russ returned to New York they were flat broke. Russ's parents met them at the JFK airport and took them to a popular restaurant at Jones Beach on Long Island; in the early hours after a noon rush the restaurant was not at full capacity. He said it's funny what a person remembers: after a wait to be seated and a very long wait for their menus they got up to leave just as the waitress appeared. About to leave again after another long wait, she reappeared to take their order. Another long wait for an unmemorable meal preceded a long wait for the bill which was to be paid to the waitress, but she was nowhere to be found. Russ's father finally paid the bill, putting money on the table with a small tip. Exiting the restaurant, the waitress suddenly made a prompt appearance, charging after them at the door shouting that in New York an appropriate tip amounted to twenty percent of the bill. They ignored her and went merrily on their way, leaving the fuming waitress standing at the exit holding the bill and the money that included the very, very modest tip. Her unresponsive attention toward them followed by her harsh rhetoric at the exit contrasted sharply to the quiet, dignified manner of the people Russ and Ron encountered in England.

In October and December, the spirit of the American people seemed to be revived by the successful Apollo missions; Apollo 8 circled the moon and returned not long after Republican Richard Nixon won the presidential election, defeating the democratic candidate, Hubert Humphrey. Ron was twenty-one and was able to cast a ballot in a presidential election year for the first time, voting for the losing Democrat. Because he had sung at the wedding of his Kent roommate, Ron was invited to his home and asked to try out for lead singer in his band. Not yet able to purchase his own vehicle, his father let him use his pickup truck for the drive to Lorain. It was a snowy weekend in December. The intended eighty-mile trip ended two miles north of Bucyrus when Ron failed to control the truck on the "black-ice" highway; the truck slid off the road into a ditch. Unhurt, Ron's first thought immediately went to the dented truck; it would need some minor repairs plus there would be a cost for pulling it from the ditch. When the Highway Patrol arrived, his apprehension grew when he was allowed to call his father. To his astonishment, the first words he uttered were not the expected reprimands; instead, he asked ,"Are you all right?" Ron didn't ever remember his father (or his mother, for that matter) saying they loved him. He never missed or needed to hear the words because of the way he was raised. But when the accident occurred, he realized his father was genuinely worried for his well-being. The concern in his voice touched him deeply. However, his visit to Lorain was postponed as was singing in his friend's band. They never got together again.

His incomplete grades in one quarter at Kent and the internship in New York delayed his graduation until April 1969. But carrying a full load of classes in that last quarter left him five credit hours short of his graduation requirements. His off-campus housemate was still teaching as an assistant for a geometry class. Whether it was his idea or proposed by his roommate remains a foggy memory, but his roommate agreed to give him a C grade without his ever attending a class. The extra credits enabled him to graduate that spring. It's doubtful his graduation that year or in the near future would have happened without those additional credits. Graduating from Kent with a C+ average ended a dubiously successful, if not sometimes stressful, period in his life. Before the graduation ceremony, his uncle Jim died of cancer at the age of forty-seven, the onset of which was said by some to be the result of his first contracting malaria during service in World War II. He was his father's best friend in high school and his mother's brother, next oldest to her in age; their interrelationship undoubtedly led to his parent's marriage. Ron's father was the oldest of four children. His mother was the oldest of five children and her brother's death was Ron's first experience of having a close relative pass away. A year later his maternal grandfather, father of his Uncle Jim, died at the age of eighty-five while Ron was serving in the army.

Another outcome of having incomplete grades one quarter at Kent was the temporary loss of his IV-F college deferment for induction in the army. His draft board deemed him 1-A—available to be drafted until a new review returned him to IV-F. It was granted, but a dispute with the woman heading the board's registration process—again his recollection of the disagreement has faded over time—provoked her to advise him that on the day of his graduation from Kent his deferment would cease. As she had promised, Ron arrived home from the graduation ceremony and in the mail a "greeting" notice from the army informed him of his induction. The army had drafted him to serve a two-year enlistment. How, or if, the woman coordinated the induction was unknown. The army notice required him to report to Fort Hayes in Columbus and from there be transferred to basic training at Fort Jackson, South Carolina. Ron was conflicted about anti-war demonstrations occurring at the time in many cities across the United States. He was sympathetic to calls for ending the war; his appeal to the draft board for a deferment, citing farm work as a reason, delayed his entry into the army by several months. He briefly considered claiming conscientious objector status but was not comfortable with that option and not sure he agreed with the demonstrators. As it turned out, his appeal was denied and he reluctantly entered the army in August 1969, a month following the historic Apollo 11 moon landing.

On September 14, the Selective Service introduced the first draft lottery while Ron was in basic training. His number would have been very high, something like 345; an induction delay of another month or two would have kept him from having to serve. He has few fond memories of his time in basic training. Unable to be helped by a tentmate suffering from some unremembered condition, he broke his eyeglasses while pitching a tent in the rain at night after one daylong march. (He apparently inherited his father's limited eyesight gene. Lenses first used before he started junior high school corrected his vision). He enjoyed assignments to drive both a guard duty jeep and a two-and-one-half ton transport truck—carrying trainees from one location to another—probably selected by the unit officer to drive because his civilian record showed him operating a similar sized truck for his father. The overnight jeep duty was okay until he negligently crumpled his issued driver's license in his khaki shirt pocket; the careless act resulted in his being placed on KP (kitchen police), peeling potatoes all next day with no intervening sleep. On the shooting range he and his foxhole buddies agreed to falsify their scores to expert; the falsified score is shown on his discharge papers. Never having exercised in his life, he was among several men who were in bad shape, but by grit and determination, and a little leniency at times by the drill instructor, he was able to complete all the necessary field work and training exercises. After the group completed basic training, many of them went to Columbia, the capital city adjacent to the base, and visited a house of ill repute. Ron said his nervous fear of interacting with women, plus their bodacious proclivities, made him unable to engage with them.

Ron, far right in picture, end of third row, circa 1969

After basic training most of the men in his unit were assigned to the infantry, but Ron was transferred to the 175th Financial Unit of the Fourth U.S. Army, 1st Armored Division, at Fort Hood, Texas, probably because of his college accounting degree. It turned out to be as easy a job as one could hope for in the army. He and other new assignees were trained as finance clerks by the previous men in their position who were then shipped to Vietnam. After about nine months their group trained another group of clerks. Those men were then shipped out too, presumably to Vietnam, while Ron's unit stayed at Fort Hood. Their jobs as finance clerks should have been safe even if destined for Vietnam, but no one in the unit wanted to go overseas into a potential harm's way assignment. They never knew why their unit had been passed over for probable overseas duty, but it might have been the result of President Nixon's pledge of "peace with honor" made in his inaugural address in 1969. To that end, he began the withdrawal of troops: 35,000 men came home in September followed by another 50,000 in December. The withdrawal continued in April 1970 when another 150,000 troops came home. A new development heard little about at the time was the first computer links being established that would lead to the creation of a new form of communication—the internet.

Drinking alcohol in moderation with some of his barracks buddies became a common weekend activity. Spurred on by his colleagues, he briefly experimented with marijuana. He accompanied one of his bunkmates to a "Boys Town" bordello one weekend in Nueva Laredo, Mexico, across the border from Laredo, Texas. The bunkmate always talked about his fabulous LSD trips. After visiting the brothel, Ron failed once again to engage with any of the women and he got drunk. Meanwhile, a man offered his bunkmate a couple of LSD tablets. In his inebriated stupor Ron plucked one from the man's grasp and swallowed it down thinking it would be a good way to prove all the stories his friend had told him were false. His friend took a tablet also and later admitted it was his worst LSD trip, saying it must have been tainted with a bad mixture of ingredients. The experience definitely increased Ron's feelings of insecurity. His knowledge about the drug was next to nothing and the experiment was terrible; it gave rise to a frightening, almost suicidal reaction. His eyes saw strange sights and his mind imagined confusing things. After the bad trip, his experimentation with drugs ceased. He feels that the use of LSD may have led to some future mental issues but that was never proved or disproved.

On other weekends away from the base there were some enjoyable times. Four of them found a golf course bordering a lake near Temple, Texas, and went there often, always stopping on the way back to dine at a restaurant that served steak and catfish dinners. When they knew they were going to the golf course for the last time, they rented a row boat across the lake and spent the day in the warm water retrieving many golf balls they and others had lost on previous trips. Along with several other men in his unit, Ron went to Houston a couple of times to see the Astros play indoor baseball games at the Astrodome, the only domed stadium at that time. Ron's concern about playing baseball under a roof changed after their visits; he enjoyed the game, the indoor setting and, more particularly, the deli sandwiches. The ill-fated flight of Apollo 13 had everyone on pins and needles until the space capsule splashed down safely in April 1970.

A more surreal episode for Ron that year was the May 4 uprising at Kent State that resulted in the deaths of four individuals; it left him dumbfounded. All his days at Kent had been peaceful without a hint of violence; a riot leading to campus deaths was incomprehensible and difficult for him to understand. Many of the men in his unit also wanted to know how it could have happened, but he could give them no plausible explanation. As members of the armed forces, they were isolated from the massive demonstrations occurring in many cities. The Kent State tragedy is still representative of an atypical episode to him. The Ohio National Guard was deployed to quell the unrest that included setting fire to the campus ROTC building, but the situation evolved to the point a guardsman opened fire on students resulting in the heartbreaking outcome. It was determined later that activists not enrolled at Kent had energized some of the student body to participate in the protests. In October his selection to work special duty as cost and budget clerk in the Headquarter III Corps Maintenance Division excluded him from most required duties: compulsory morning roll call, routine inspections and standing guard duty. His only military requirement was to continue wearing his fatigue uniform. Other than that nothing distinguished him from the other mostly civilian employees at the maintenance division; he worked nine to five for the rest of his tour of duty.

The next year, troop withdrawals from Vietnam continued with more men being returned to the United States. A troop reduction called for by the Selective Service bill allowed for an early release from the army of up to four months for certain soldiers. Word circulated in their unit that a three-month early release application might be approved. Those not intending to reenlist filed an application and most were granted. The request for early release required justification and it was an unexpected surprise that his application to work on his parent's farm was approved. A similar request had been denied at the time of his induction. His father didn't need any help, but Ron's discharge came through with no questions asked. His twenty-one-month tour of duty ended in May 1971. After working his last eight months on special duty, D.W. Jones LTC, OrdC chief of the Maintenance Division, gave him an excellent Letter of Appreciation upon his release from the division. Ron said the letter embarrassed him because his performance and attitude while working there did not justify its fine words. Actually, he said, a great deal of his time was spent ogling at the lieutenant colonel's attractive secretary. Although his unit was fairly close-knit, he did not stay in touch with anyone after his discharge.

Following his tour of duty with the army, he returned home to fulfill his farm work discharge requirement and managed to muster up enough courage to date a former high school classmate that summer—the first dates since his ill-fated one in college. They went out together a couple of times before she returned to fall quarter graduate classes at The Ohio State University in Columbus. He had driven his parent's car on their dates but after she left, he was eager to purchase his first car. So, at age 24, relying on accrued leave and sick balances paid to him by the army plus unemployment benefits, he had enough money to buy a 1968 Volkswagen Beetle. By the following year, sales of the Volkswagen Beetle would exceed those of the Ford Model-T.

After spending three months on the farm home with his parents, Ron searched for employment and found a job and an apartment in Upper Sandusky, Ohio, about eight miles west of Nevada. He worked several months operating an extrusion molding machine in a factory fashioning plastic bead into component parts used in various products. Soon disillusioned by his job, and because his friend Don and the girl he dated had returned to Ohio State, he decided to enroll there for the 1972 winter quarter. He was able to get a room in the same off-campus house Don lived in but decided there was no future for him and his "girlfriend"; she moaned deeply when he ended their relationship. It was an emotional moment, and for many years he thought of that last time in her Jones Tower room, hearing her sigh of regret because he wanted to end their brief flirtation. Much later it came to him her exhalation was probably more a sigh of relief that she would no longer have to see him; undoubtedly, she already had moved on with her life anyway, not having seen him for several months. His enrollment at Ohio State was funded by the army GI Bill program, but with no desire to continue furthering his education and because the relationship with the woman had ended, he decided it was time for him to go back to work.

Ron returned to another Upper Sandusky apartment house with no definite plan for the future but his move was not without its rewards. He was hired by Continental Hydraulic Hose Corporation to be its quality control inspector. Working for the brake hose manufacturer was a new challenge, as was working with the unique personalities of the five owners at the small plant. One of the owners trained him for the new job and Ron generally enjoyed the responsibility of certifying the brake components met the necessary standards. Current events such as the escalating conflict between the United Kingdom and Northern Ireland, the Watergate break-in in Washington, DC, and the last ground troops leaving Vietnam went under his radar. As the year went on, other events did attract his attention. The world was astonished when Palestinian terrorists kidnapped nine Israeli athletes, leading to their deaths, during the Olympic Games in Munich. At the end of September, in the last regular season baseball game for the Pittsburgh Pirates, Roberto Clemente got the three-thousandth hit of his career and joined only ten other players at the time with at least that many lifetime hits. From Puerto Rico, he was the first Latin American player to reach that plateau. Many baseball fans and others were shocked when he died that winter in a plane that crashed while attempting to carry relief aid to victims of the Managua, Nicaragua, earthquake. In November, Richard Nixon—Ron voted for him this time—was reelected president and in December Apollo 17, the last flight to land men on the moon, was launched and returned safely to earth.

Ron's first-ever employment vacation was an adventurous cross-country drive to the coast of California in July 1973. Driving his VW Beetle cross-country, the itinerary ended at the coastline highway along the Pacific Ocean. On his return to Ohio, the southern rim of the Grand Canyon proved to be an awesome stopover. The grand expanse of the country was inspiring but tempered by the fact no one was with him to share the experience. On the last long sloping road exiting the Rocky Mountains, the brakes on the VW went out but rebooted as he limped into a town at the base of the mountains. After several stop-and-go sessions, the brakes seemed to be fine. He thought they had probably overheated on the road. It would take him more than a year to find out air in the brake line, probably the result of his continuous braking on the long descent down from the mountains, had caused the problem.

While working at the brake hose manufacturer, he took notice of one of the female employees. She was a cute woman; a single mother working on a crimping machine. Still leading a solitary lifestyle, his attempt to establish a relationship with her were rejected. A short canoe trip down the Sandusky River to the Indian Mill Museum near Upper Sandusky one day was the only time they spent a significant amount of time together away from the plant. Marriage was not on his mind, and after working at the plant for a year and a half, and disillusioned by his failure to have a relationship with her or any other woman, he decided to quit his job and move to Columbus. He was hired for a Nationwide Insurance job training program, but within a week one of his former employers at the brake hose manufacturer approached him with an offer to be manager at another plant they owned in Michigan near Detroit. The opportunity to manage Rochester Precision Parts Corporation, and the $12,000 salary, was too great to resist, and Rochester,

Michigan, became his new home. As manager of the small screw machine plant his work included ordering material and acting as supervisor to the fifteen employees as well as updating job pricing cost sheets for parts sold to various manufacturers. The job pricing task aligned with his accounting schooling; in developing new cost sheets he found much of their sale products were grossly underpriced.

Ron remembers Mack Truck as the main purchaser of their parts and most of the material bought for machining came from Central Steel and Wire. The salesman for Central Steel gave Ron and a fellow co-worker several tips on where to dine and tickets for a few sporting events. Ron and his co-worker drove to Cleveland one weekend to attend the boxing match between Muhammad Ali and Chuck Wepner. The fight went fifteen rounds with no knockdowns although Wepner stepped on Ali's foot once late in the fight causing him to fall. Ali was awarded the decision on a TKO in the last round. Sitting well back from the ring, it was hard to tell if the blows each fighter made were doing any damage. When the fight was over, the two boxers walked down the exit aisle past Ron. Wepner had to be supported by two handlers on either side so he wouldn't fall, and his face looked like hamburger. On the other hand, Ali walked briskly, unattended by anyone; his face was unmarked and he was grinning broadly.

On his way to begin work in Rochester, Ron approached an intersection on a Detroit boulevard and as he attempted to brake, his foot went to the floor. With cars blocking all lanes ahead of him at a traffic light and wanting to avoid a rear-end collision, he steered the car onto the grassy section of the boulevard hoping to stop it by downshifting into a lower gear but the car hurtled through cross-traffic lanes, incredibly encountering no intersecting traffic. The car continued on to the grass divider on the other side of the road before rolling to a stop. After testing the brakes, the car seemed to operate fine, but the brake issues prompted him to search for a new car. He purchased a low mileage 1964 Plymouth Valiant, operated by a push-button drive transmission. Sometime later an employee at the precision parts factory bought the VW from him at a minimal price. The employee heeded Ron's warning about its braking problems but declared the car fixed and good as new after the simple process of bleeding air out of the brake lines. However, the Valiant was much roomier and more comfortable to drive than the Volkswagen and turned out to be one of his favorite vehicles.

Trying to establish a relationship before moving to Columbus, followed by another move to Michigan near the end of the year, caused Ron to mostly ignore current events. In January 1973 the beginning of the trial of the suspects in the Watergate break-in took place, the landmark decision Roe v. Wade legalizing elective abortion came later as did the announcement by President Nixon of a Vietnam peace accord. The World Trade Center was officially dedicated in April; America's first space station, designated Skylab, was launched in May; and by June, Secretariat had established himself as one of the greatest thoroughbred horses in history with record-breaking times in the Triple Crown races. The Senate Watergate hearings were being conducted and in July the White House tapes recorded by President Nixon during the break-in were subpoenaed. The involvement by the president in Watergate and its potential scandal first came to Ron's attention with the resignation of many of his top aides at the end of April. Other embarrassing aspects of the Nixon administration became apparent when Vice President Agnew resigned in October after being accused of tax evasion. Gerald Ford was confirmed by the House of Representatives near the end of the year to be the new vice president. His confirmation did not quiet the growing discontent.

CHAPTER 5
1974-1976

Ron was employed at Rochester Precision Parts from late 1973 through the first half of 1975. After working there for several months, one of the owners took him on a sales trip, flying from Detroit to Chicago, Tulsa, Oklahoma, and on to Fort Worth, Texas, before returning to Michigan. In February 1974, his maternal grandmother died at the age of eighty; the funeral was in Nevada but because of the distance to travel in inclement weather Ron did not return from Michigan to attend the services. In April he vacationed in Guatemala, visiting his cousin working as a Peace Corps volunteer.

After his return, a co-worker at Rochester Precision introduced him to a woman living in his apartment building, and at the age of twenty-seven Ron became involved in his first intimate relationship. She was almost his height, attractive, dark-haired and with a slim figure; several years junior to him, she still had braces on her teeth, which were removed during the course of their time together. It was primarily a physical relationship but they enjoyed each other's company for most of the rest of the year, going to festivals, an Andy Williams concert and to a drive-in movie once or twice.

Exploring sexuality and intimacy, they ignored much of the other happenings of the year including the impeachment hearings of President Nixon and the order by the Supreme Court for him to release the White House tapes. When he gave his final speech resigning the presidency in August, they were in a hotel room after driving to Toronto for a long weekend. Even Ford's ascension to the presidency and his subsequent pardon of Nixon didn't interrupt their infatuation with one another. Ron did watch the so-called "Rumble in the Jungle"—the heavyweight title match between Muhammad Ali and George Foreman—at the end of October. His hope for a Foreman victory was quashed by Ali's rope-a-dope tactics. In December the House of Representatives confirmed Nelson Rockefeller to be vice president.

The relationship with the woman began to unwind one day beginning with a trivial incident. Returning to her apartment she reprimanded him for carelessly releasing the brake pedal after stopping her car. Ron believed she was growing increasingly frustrated with him because he seemed to be content with a physical relationship. She had introduced him to her parents when they made a surprise visit to her apartment and then, after suggesting marriage as a possibility, she also confessed to a previous encounter with a married man. Her honest, open admission stirred up in him emotions of envy and jealousy, thinking if she had other intimate relationships he was entitled to have them too. His impulse to end what had been a loving, caring time together was foolish and insensitive but to say he loved her wouldn't be accurate either. By the end of the year their relationship had dissolved and Ron was alone once again.

Probably remembering his visit to Guatemala to see his cousin, Ron's next step was to join the Peace Corps. After completing an application process, he was accepted to depart in July 1975 to Malaysia. Two events in April of that year should be noted: Bill Gates and a partner founded Microsoft, and the last evacuees from Vietnam ended the United States involvement in that country. Before Ron left for Malaysia, a singular event took place that was destined to be as adventurous as his Peace Corps experience. His friend Don contacted him in Michigan. They both had recently purchased motorcycles and Don suggested visiting their friend Russ, his companion in England, who had joined the Peace Corps in El Salvador.

After giving a two-week notice to leave his position with Rochester Precision Parts, Ron joined Don gathering up gear for their journey. They set off one day in late May without a care in the world except Ron had to return in time for his Peace Corps departure. The trip was quickly decided and had all the earmarks of potential trouble. Neither one of them had what would be considered a long-distance touring bike; both were smaller 350cc models, Don had a Suzuki and Ron had purchased a Honda. Leaving Ohio, they drove south through Kentucky, Tennessee, Arkansas and a long two-day journey across Texas before reaching Mexico at Laredo. In 1975 only visas were required to cross borders into Mexico, Guatemala, and El Salvador. In Mexico, they passed through Monterrey and on to Oaxaca by way of Tampico and Veracruz on the east coast, sometimes getting behind a truck in the night to navigate hard rain on dark roads.

Ron, on his 350cc Honda motorcycle, somewhere in Mexico, circa 1975

Southern Mexico had high mountain meadows and a couple of spectacular waterfalls before the highlands of Guatemala were crossed, notable for remarkable scenery and extinct volcanoes. El Salvador has a rich, diverse landscape too, but passing through these two countries left Ron with no outstanding memories. They met Russ and his future wife in a small village where she lived. The people of the village all were friendly and seemed to have a comfortable lifestyle even though there were few conveniences. His most enduring memory in El Salvador was when they drove to the west coast to frolic in the Pacific Ocean.

From left to right, Ron, Russ (on horse), and Don, circa 1975

Their return trip was notable for several events. Ron said one time he was driving fast and failed to negotiate a curve. He crossed over into the opposite lane of traffic and an oncoming car had to swerve to avoid him. In Oaxaca, they discovered a former residence of John Steinbeck. In the same city, they came upon a small church filled with a myriad of candles burning on the altar and throughout the interior. It was a stunning sight. They never knew its significance. Later, Ron learned it was about this time his paternal grandfather had died. When they were approaching Veracruz both their bikes began to give them trouble. The compression on Don's engine had diminished and Ron's engine conked out. He said it got low on oil due to his negligence; the engine seized and became inoperable. It was late in the day and they were about ten miles from Veracruz. Don said he would go on to the city, rent a car, and come back for him as soon as he could. Shortly after he drove away a man drove up on a mini-bike. He was a local and spoke only Spanish, but Ron tried, with his limited language skills, to communicate with him; he was offering to tow Ron into the city. He pulled out a frayed piece of twine and attached it to both bikes. He didn't see Ron smile at the futility of his effort. The man's bike was small compared to his Honda and the condition of the rope was questionable, but the man's instincts were better than those of Ron—he pulled him right into the city center of Veracruz, arriving after dark; the man refused to take any money for his efforts.

    Once in Veracruz, Ron tried to find Don; they had not passed him on the road to the city so his first instinct was to search for a hotel Don might have stayed in until the next morning. His effort was rewarded after a several hour search. A clerk at a hotel near the gulf coast waters said Don was registered but would not disclose his room number. It was approaching three in the morning and after a futile argument Ron returned to the nearby park to try and get some sleep on one of its benches; the inflated room charge for a short night and a deflated wallet kept Ron from registering for a room. It was his good fortune that as the morning sun appeared above the horizon he saw Don driving a rental car on the street next to the park. Ron was able to flag him down or he would have driven back to the place he left him the day before and they may never have reconnected. As he remembers it, they sold their disabled bikes for a minimal price to some guys at a mechanic shop on a side street and then caught a bus from Veracruz to Matamoros, across the border from Brownsville, Texas. A Greyhound bus took them back to Ohio.

Soon after returning to Ohio, Ron began his Peace Corps assignment. He sold the Plymouth Valiant to a former high school acquaintance and joined his cousin (the brother of his cousin in Guatemala) who had also been accepted for a Peace Corps assignment in Malaysia. They united with other volunteers on a plane to San Francisco and a tour of the city for a day or two before their overseas flight to Kuala Lumpur, the capital city of Malaysia, with a brief stopover in Tokyo. In Kuala Lumpur, their group of twenty or thirty volunteers were sent to different training locations. His cousin was in a group that went to southern Malaysia while other volunteers, including Ron, were in a group that traveled to the east coast city of Kuantan. They were scheduled to do about two months of language training in country before going on to a permanent placement. The many volunteers all had different knowledge they hoped to impart but because of his farm background Ron had been assigned to be an agricultural maintenance specialist; that so-called expertise would take him to a farm near the west coast of the country to work on a ranch being carved out of the jungle. The Peace Corps proved to be a more difficult and lengthy adventure than the monthlong free-riding trip through Mexico.

Malaysia is a tropical country with some beautiful beaches; towns and villages dot the coastal plains. The center of the country is mountainous jungle with few populated areas. Its consistently warm temperatures range from an average low of seventy degrees to an average high of over ninety degrees with high humidity. In 1975, ethnic Malays (mostly Muslims) comprised about 60 percent of the total population, Chinese 28 percent and Indians 9 percent. Ron and the fifteen or so volunteers that traveled to the east coast began to experience the culture of the country while participating in daily language training. In the middle of their training they were each assigned to spend two weeks with a village family in order to better familiarize themselves with the people and the language.

It was a challenging experience and several volunteers opted to return to the United States. Ron's language deficiencies were always a problem; acquiring the communication skills necessary to carry on a conversation was always a struggle for him. Fortunately, most of the young people in the village and, later, the men working on the farm, wanted to speak English.

His village assignment while in training took him to the rustic home of Pak Chik Soro and Mak Chik Citi, roughly equivalent to grandpa and grandma Chik, who kept a home, which was supported on stilts, for several of their grandchildren.

Ron with Chik family
Pak Chik and Mak Chik identified by arrows

Chik family home

His clothing consisted of a shirt, sarong, and sandals. The family usually ate rice with fish in bowls placed on a floor mat; a thin mattress on a raised wooden plank was his bed. An outside well was the bathing area for everyone, soaping their bodies through the sarong. A rudimentary toilet, similar to the old outhouse on his parents' rented farm, was positioned many yards from the house. During the day the people went to jobs in Kuantan or other towns; he does not remember his daytime activities but various chores and language study probably kept him busy; it was a peaceful, rewarding time except for worries about speaking the Malay language. The grown children of the Chik's lived nearby and one of their sons had the only television in the village; many people came to his house to watch the government-controlled programming, shown only in the evening. News broadcasts were followed by popular sitcoms or variety shows that always ended with the playing of the country national anthem over an image of the Malaysian flag and a flyover of their air force jets.

In September, during their language training, two assassination attempts on President Ford were thwarted in California. The attempts on Ford were reported in the newspapers, but no mention of the *Saturday Night Live* comedy sketch that debuted on NBC ever reached their ears. Ron was disappointed, but not overly so, that he missed what came to be referred to as one of the greatest World Series ever played. Cincinnati beat Boston in seven games. The training in Kuantan included operating bulldozers used to topple jungle trees and foliage at the developing farms, but his placement at the agricultural station located near the village of Tajung Malim, about eighty miles north of Kuala Lumpur, did not require him to use one. The farm was one of several developing 5,000-acre sites designated as Majuternak, the state livestock development corporation.

Ron, top row left, on Majuternak farm with other employees, circa 1975

He and another volunteer at the farm discussed projects with the manager. They decided an equipment maintenance schedule for the tractors and other equipment on the farm was needed and a workshop should be built and stocked with tools. A nice house on top of a hill overlooking the farm was provided for them next to a house occupied by a couple from New Zealand. The husband was being paid to establish a herd of dairy cattle, which accounted for about 15 percent of the livestock on the farm, the remaining 85 percent being beef cattle.

At first Ron spent time assisting the man from New Zealand, one time helping him tie a rope to the legs of a calf to pull it from the mother cow's birth canal. He helped him set up milking stall equipment in the dairy barns and assisted him at the farm water tanks, chlorinating the water supply and treating it with softeners. His wife cooked some savory meals and provided welcome female perspectives. Ron's first few weeks were also spent getting to know several of the farm supervisors: a Malay, a Chinese, and two Indian men, coincidentally represented the cultural diversity of the country. As the weeks went on, they would drive to Tajung Malim in a farm jeep and dine in a café/restaurant unique to each of their cultures. Chinese food was familiar to Ron and he had dined on Malay food in Kuantan and at his village placement. However, the Indian food was a new treat; various meats (lamb, beef and fish) accompanied rice served on banana leaves along with Indian flat bread baked on a circular grill. These meals were probably his favorite but with all the choices none of them went hungry. As the weeks went by, Ron became intoxicated on some of these trips to town. When that happened, his more sober companions helped him return safely to the farm.

During the year he worked at the ranch several things stood out in his memory: monkeys carousing high in the tree tops; being followed by a gigantic monitor lizard on a jungle lane one day, glad to be on the farm tractor; seeing a wild hog run into a bamboo shelter near the edge of the jungle (tigers were seen at times on farms, but he never saw one); visiting a rubber plantation to watch the milk-colored sap collect in cups attached to the trees. He was invited for a weekend visit to the west coast home of the Malay farm supervisor and went with him to the island of Penang. He and Louie, another volunteer, went on a two-week vacation to Thailand. They went by train to Bangkok and continued on from there to visit Angor What, the Bridge on the River Kwai, and Chiang Mai, a city in the northern part of the country close to the Chinese border. In Chiang Mai, Louie was shot in the leg during an argument with a local man while Ron dallied with a female. Louie said the man pointed the gun at his chest but he was able to push it down the moment the shot was fired. Ron helped him get to a hospital where he spent a recovery day while being treated for his wound. On other excursions, they visited Singapore at the time of the 1976 Chinese New Year and played golf on a nine-hole course in the cool central highland resort of Fraser's Hill. After years of sending yearly greetings, they eventually lost touch. Ron was saddened to learn Louie died in 2018.

After Ron's first weeks on the farm, he went to Kuala Lumpur to purchase a motorcycle—he bought a British-manufactured Norton model. He said it wasn't the most reliable bike he had owned, but when it was running properly it gave him an occasion for independent travel; local buses did not run on his schedule. On some weekends he drove to Kuala Lumpur to get a taste of city life and get away from the farm. While in the city he spent some of his time looking, and occasionally paying, for female companionship. With the help of the other volunteer on the farm, a Malay worker was trained to implement the maintenance schedule. They constructed the workshop one hot day under the pole barns where the tractors were parked. The shop walls were put up after mixing and pouring a concrete floor by hand. It was the most difficult job they undertook on the farm. After the workshop was finished it was stocked with tools they purchased in Kuala Lumpur.

When his work assignment at the farm was complete, Ron was asked to transfer to another farm, but because he was still unable to feel comfortable speaking the Malay language, and because of a general frustration with the program, he decided to terminate his two-year commitment after fourteen months. Factoring into his decision were rumblings of dissatisfaction voiced to Ron by the farm manager. Being a proud citizen of the country, the manager insisted Malaysia did not need foreign aid or assistance in the form of the Peace Corps. Ron's decision to not transfer to a new work assignment was met with criticism from the country director.

However, during a discussion with him, Ron pointed out quite a few volunteers to the country did not survive even two months of language training and enjoyed the equivalent of a vacation before returning home. That settled the argument, at least for Ron. The sale of his motorcycle and his last meager paycheck didn't amount to much but it added up to enough money for a ticket to Hawaii. As a side note, Peace Corps volunteers served in Malaysia twenty-one years, 1962-1983. Although beef and dairy cattle are still being developed, 1983 also marked the end of the Majuternak program. A volunteer who worked in Malaysia at the same time as Ron returned to the country thirty years later. She told him all eight Majuternak farms were abandoned and jungle growth had overtaken the farm land.

Hawaii was a brief, beautiful interval. Arriving in the capital city of Honolulu on the island of Oahu with no funds, Ron called his parents and asked them to wire him enough money to get home. His attempt to spend the first night in a joy house failed and sleeping on Waikiki beach was illegal so he wandered about the city the first night. He received the money requested from his parents the next day, bought an airline ticket, and then rented a car and drove around Oahu, exploring pineapple plantations and beaches on the north shore. After an all too short stay, he returned to Ohio. With no offers of work and without a plan—a common theme in his life—his father suggested a job opening with the Crawford County Producers Livestock Cooperative might be available. His father knew their office manager was retiring and thought it would be a good opportunity. Although not excited about the job, Ron's resources were low and there seemed to be no better options. After moving to an apartment in a Bucyrus home, his life returned to a form of normalcy. He earned enough money to buy a car—a 1968 Chevy Impala—and a previously owned Honda motorcycle. The Bucyrus cooperative was okay at first but soon one of his co-workers began comparing him in a negative way to the man he replaced. He tried to be cordial with her and they managed to work together in a pleasant way for a while.

He didn't try to contact former friends at first; connecting with someone he hadn't seen for over two years to renew old acquaintances did not appeal to him. But after a few months he contacted Don who was teaching disabled children in Cincinnati and dating a woman from Columbus. Don introduced him to his girlfriend and her roommate; the four of them visited Miami University together and on a long weekend traveled to New Orleans. The roommate was engaged to be married, but in the brief time they spent together Ron became attracted to her, probably because he was lonely for female companionship. He stopped in Columbus another time and stayed overnight at her apartment before continuing on to Cincinnati to stay with Don. Not long after that, she unexpectedly came to visit them. The night before her visit he and Don went to a strip club across the Ohio River in Covington, Kentucky, and coaxed one of their dancers to return to Don's apartment with them. The African-American woman didn't refuse Ron's advances, but following their intimate act Ron said the inside of his head seemed to spark colorful shooting stars, in a way reminiscent of sensations triggered by his LSD trip in the army. He felt uncomfortable afterwards and it may have been predictive of future events.

Ron's encounter with the dancer caused him to have a profound sense of guilt when the roommate arrived the next day; paying for sex instead of trying to form a closer bond with her disturbed him greatly and caused him to, once again, assess his inability to form meaningful relationships, especially with the opposite sex; those thoughts triggered some disturbing episodes. Soon after returning to Bucyrus, restless and sleepless nights while thinking about his conduct began to plague him. In the middle of one night, he walked to a nearby church hoping to get some help or direction but as far as he knew his call to God went unanswered. The next morning at work he looked in a washroom mirror and in a hallucination his reflection resembled the painting of the man in the movie *The Picture of Dorian Gray*. Ron collapsed and a co-worker found him on the floor and phoned his mother. She took him to the pastor of the

Lutheran church but he was unable to help. With no other apparent recourse, she asked the Richland County Psychiatric Hospital near Mansfield, Ohio, to admit him as a patient. It must have been quite a strain for her. She had a daughter diagnosed with schizophrenia living at home and now her only other child was going for psychiatric care too. Ron has only a few vague memories of his time in the hospital the last several months of the year. He does remember he was discharged in time to vote for Gerald Ford in the presidential election in November that was won by Jimmy Carter.

CHAPTER 6
1977-1984

In January 1977, Apple Computer, formed by Steve Jobs and partners the previous year, was incorporated. The space shuttle had its maiden flight in August after a February test ride aboard a Boeing 747 aircraft. And in July, fifteen countries, including the United States, the Soviet Union, and the United Kingdom, signed a nuclear non-proliferation pact. All those achievements went unnoticed by Ron. He had recently turned thirty and his release from the hospital near the end of the previous year came with no diagnosis or medication. His employment with the livestock cooperative was terminated. Fortunately, he had submitted an application to work at Yosemite National Park a few months prior to his hospitalization. His Peace Corps experience on the application turned out to be beneficial because the hiring manager at Yosemite was also a former Peace Corps volunteer and his application was approved; he was hired to join the office staff at the park for the summer. After Ron's journey to California, the manager received no acknowledgement from Ron of their shared experience, probably disappointing the manager as much as it saddened Ron. His self-worth was at a low point and he avoided interacting with him except for work-related matters.

Upon accepting the position at Yosemite, Ron drove his Chevy Impala cross-country towing his motorcycle behind him in a U-Haul trailer. In Indiana his westward progress seemed to take a turn for the worse. Running out of gas on a highway off ramp at night was not on his agenda. After coasting to a stop well off the road, his walk to a nearby gas station for a can of fuel took only a few minutes but in the interim the car was sideswiped; the entire left side was dented in and scratched. A driver of another car waited for him to return and informed Ron a semi-truck did the damage and kept on going after the collision. He had even written down the license number of the truck. After Ron arrived at Yosemite his claim to his insurer for compensation was honored, but he pocketed the cash and repaired the damages himself as best he could. Continuing on from the accident scene was difficult. In his fragile state of mind, he began talking periodically to an imaginary person in the back seat of his car to try and calm his nerves. He said it didn't help much.

Yosemite Falls, circa 1977

Yosemite was a wonderful interlude, although working in the payroll office that summer was slightly stressful for Ron; he was still recovering from the realization he had had some kind of mental breakdown that required hospitalization. Sharing a tent with another employee for their living quarters was uncomfortable too; his living arrangements were rugged to say the least but common shower and dining hall facilities were available. Most of his non-work time during the week was spent at the park library or in the recreation hall, returning to the tent at bedtime. Almost immediately after getting settled, he met a woman co-worker who became a friend. She suspected his insecurity and a relationship never developed, but they often explored the park together. One long weekend she and another co-worker and Ron decided to hike to the Hetch-Hetchy valley near the reservoir in the northwest corner of the park. They carried a tent and sleeping bags along with sufficient food and water for a couple of nights. It was bear country so preventive bear measures were practiced, including hoisting the food up in a bag between two trees and propping their backpacks against a tree well away from the tent. But as luck would have it, the first night a bear visited their camp and was not to be deterred. It got the bag, ate their food, and continued to penetrate all their toothpaste canisters and punctured all but one of their water bottles in the backpacks. The next day they hiked back to Yosemite Valley sharing the one remaining water bottle and, mercifully, came upon a roadside restaurant and ordered a fine steak dinner with plenty of water on the side.

    Don had moved to Los Angeles and enrolled in the American Film Institute to pursue a writing degree. His new girlfriend from Cincinnati was living in Laguna Hills, and one long weekend Ron rode his motorcycle over 380 miles one way—seven long hours—to visit her. Another weekend he drove through the night heat of Death Valley to meet Don in Las Vegas. The drive was almost the same distance as his drive to Laguna Hills and both times the exhausting travel required several days to recover after he returned to Yosemite. Ron found that a weekend daytime hike was the best way to relax and several times he drove into the Sierra Nevada ranges inside the park in order to unwind from the Monday through Friday routine. One time he and his woman friend and several other co-workers camped out overnight in the high ranges in Tuolumne Meadow under a breathlessly clear sky with a myriad of stars visible. They were able to view a satellite course its way across the sky, seeming to pass unscathed through the stars. At the end of summer, Ron was offered a permanent position working in the park. If he stayed over the cold snowy winter, he would move into spacious living quarters in a wooden bungalow with all the conveniences. He turned it down, but later thought continuing to work at the park may have been a better choice. He had decided to move to San Diego, hoping Southern California might be a good place to start over with his life.

Making new friends in San Diego, as well as in other places he had lived, was difficult. Living alone and working on his own was a familiar way of life; an apartment near Balboa Park suited his needs. When his parents called to wish him a happy birthday in 1978, they told him about the great blizzard that was sweeping through their region. It was one of the most powerful storms ever recorded in the Ohio Valley but Southern California remained warm and pleasant all winter long. His first job driving a bagel delivery truck lasted about six months. The deliveries took him all over the various communities of the city and one day each week he drove to Los Angeles to deliver bagels to a couple of restaurants. In San Diego his favorite delivery spot was at a café in Ocean Beach. The work hours began to wear on him, however. Getting up at 3:30 a.m. to get to the bakery and load the truck with freshly baked bagels to start his delivery run at 4:30 a.m. for a twelve-hour day was too tiring. Ron soon found a different job driving taxi for Diamond Cab Company in National City, just south of San Diego.

Taxi cab license, circa 1978

The daytime hours and new work environment were a welcome change but his paycheck-to-paycheck existence continued. Ron sold the Chevy Impala and bought a sportscar, a Triumph TR-3. He got it on the road a few times but it never was dependable transportation. His main mode of transportation was the motorcycle. For the next year, driving taxi was his only activity except for a daily three-mile run in the park.

In September, the crash of a Boeing 727 aircraft made headlines in San Diego after it collided with a Cessna plane while on its approach to the airport; the planes plummeted into hilltop communities not far from Ron's apartment, killing the two men in the Cessna, 135 passengers and crew on the 727, and seven people on the ground. That same month the Camp David peace accord between Israel and Egypt was signed, but the Guyana mass murders and suicides in Jonestown seemed to occupy more headlines when they took place in November.

Ron had no social life; he did not frequent bars or try to search out community events. His fear of interacting with people was a continuing problem. One night the evangelist Billy Graham had a televised crusade and asked the audience, including those watching at home, to ask Jesus Christ into their heart. His life was going nowhere so asking Christ to help him seemed to be a way out of a rut. He got on his knees and in a desperate plea asked Jesus to take over. If he could trust Christ, then he might finally be on the right path. However, his skeptical wait to be transformed into a new person did not materialize. Things began to change but not always in a good way, at least at first.

After asking Christ into his life, attending church seemed to be the next logical step. He met a new friend somewhere along the way; meeting him may have occurred at one of the churches he visited. As far as Ron could recall, they got together occasionally to go to Bible studies or just hang out. He remembered one night they were riding in his TR-3—one of the few times Ron got it on the road—and passed a dead woman lying on the interstate off-ramp. His friend stayed with the body while Ron got to a phone to call the police; after being questioned the police thanked them and said they could go their own way. Apparently, the woman had been murdered, but they never learned any more details about her death. Eventually his friend convinced him to rent a home with him. They both were attracted to a woman in a Bible study who had three younger children from a previous relationship, but Ron's judgmental instincts took over, silently condemning her for letting herself be put in the position of being a single mother, as if it was all her fault. The woman who worked at Continental Hose years earlier was also a single mom. He remembered his attitude toward her was similar and probably the reason they never bonded.

Most of Ron's taxi fares were routine, but one day after dropping off a person in San Ysidro near the Mexican border his stop for a beverage at a nearby 7-Eleven led to his most interesting fare. Two Mexican men were waiting at the cab when he returned from the store and requested a ride to Los Angeles. Ron was sure they were illegal immigrants and after calling his office to learn the protocol, he was told to accept their money—he thought it might have been two-hundred dollars—and proceed to LA. What would have happened at their destination never crossed his mind but it became a moot issue because north of La Jolla on interstate 5 his cab was flagged down and ordered to pull over at an immigration checkpoint; the men were removed from the cab. He could only surmise his office had called the checkpoint and told them the fare was on its way. The immigrants wanted their money back but it had been put in a metal safe box—company regulation to prevent robbery—which could only be opened by an office key. Ron gave them an address to contact to request a refund. He had thought it improbable they would ever write so it was quite a surprise when a month later he got a letter from them in Mexico asking for the money, which was promptly mailed back to them.

In January 1979, Ron's paternal grandmother passed away at the age of eighty-one. The close-knit families of his father and mother had become fragmented, even before the death of their last remaining parent. As with the funeral of his maternal grandmother, Ron did not return to Ohio to attend her service. Continuing to drive the cab and read the Bible every day seemed to be working out for him. He had not formed any new female relationship or made close friends with other men, but his life seemed to be on a straight course. However, one day early that year a man dressed in suit and tie carrying a Bible hailed his cab for a ride. Ron drove him to his requested destination and continued on to a distant taxi stand to wait for a call for another fare. To Ron's confused surprise, the same man, or a man who appeared to be the same, also carrying a Bible, was waiting at the stand for a ride to another location. Very few fares were solicited at a cab stand and it seemed improbable the man could have arrived at the taxi stand ahead of him, and yet there the man stood and asked for a ride to another location.

Ron was disturbed by this chain of events. After the incident sleepless nights similar to what had been his experience before leaving Ohio returned, along with apocalyptic visions and a distorted state of mind. He commandeered the woman from church with the three children on a hellish ride to a Bible study group. On another day, while clutching his Bible and wandering the streets, he shouted scripture at patrons socializing in a bar. Someone called the police and they stopped his rants and raves by slamming his head into the pavement and immediately transported him to the San Diego Hillcrest hospital where his emaciated body was treated and his tormented soul was calmed. After unremembered days he was discharged and does not recall receiving a diagnosis; a nurse explained he would probably need to take a prescribed medication, also one he no longer remembers, for the rest of his life.

After the hospitalization his friend and housemate suggested Teen Challenge, a Christian rehabilitation program for people with drug, alcohol, or other life-controlling issues, might be an appropriate place for him to go for ongoing treatment. The name Teen Challenge is misleading: it is a recovery regimen that provides care not only for teens but also for adults and families; the Christ-centered, faith-based organization referred to today as ATC—Adult & Teen Challenge—has separate facilities for men, women, and families. Ron agreed to his friend's recommendation and applied for an opening. After being accepted, he was asked to move to a Bakersfield, California, residence for a six-week preliminary assessment. The home was designed to begin a rehabilitation process to determine if a person could adhere to the rules and regulations of the program before being transferred to their main facility in Riverside, California. The only memory Ron has of his time in Bakersfield is that one of their counselors convinced him to stop taking the medication prescribed by the doctor at the hospital in San Diego and, instead, rely on Jesus to provide the needed remedy. Wanting to believe the advice of the counselor, Ron discontinued the medication.

Following the preliminary residence, he was transferred to the men's main campus in a Riverside castle for a continuing nine-month treatment course. It was an actual castle, the former home of a Riverside resident.

Teen Challenge castle, Riverside, California, circa 1979

Probably thirty men were in the program during his residency. Everyone was required to attend Bible classes on a daily basis, visit nearby church worship services to give testimony to their recovery, and assigned to do various jobs. After a two-week familiarization to the campus, Ron was assigned to be the breakfast cook for the men and staff. It was a pleasant enough chore. His staggered menu choices included cereal grains one day, another day pancakes and French toast; on other mornings various egg dishes—poached, scrambled, over easy—were served with ham, bacon, or breakfast and chorizo sausage, and hash browned potatoes. All the meals were warmly received except for the occasional bulgur cereal. Deep frying potatoes and doughnuts proved successful until one morning a large pan of oil burst into flame; the local fire department had to be called, ending future deep fryer breakfast foods.

Insulated from outside events or activities during their stay at Teen Challenge, most world proceedings were unreported. However, the first papal visit to the White House in September by John Paul II and the Iranian hostage crisis that developed in November reached their ears. Over the course of nine months at Riverside, the men studied books of the Bible and were introduced to different forms of worship—Baptist, nondenominational, Pentecostal, and charismatic services. They also discussed different religious experiences: revelational, mystical, and meditative. Ron was uncomfortable when called on to testify at the churches they attended about how Teen Challenge was helping cure him of an alcohol or drug problem. He had not used stimulants for a long time and did not know how to say he was dealing with a mental issue. Invariably he gave testimonials that were distorted or misleading as to the true nature of his problem.

At some point in the studies, the phenomena of glossolalia, or speaking in tongues, occupied the conversation of the residents. Believed by some to be a sacred language of prayer, speaking in tongues became a popular ritual for Ron and the other men for a period of time. Glossolalia is defined as the fluid vocalizing of speech-like syllables lacking any readily comprehended meaning. It could also mean the supposed speaking of a natural language previously unknown to the speaker. In the Bible, Paul writes in his first letter to the Corinthians (14:2) his spirit was cheered because: "For anyone who speaks in a tongue does not speak to men but to God. Indeed, no one understands him; he utters mysteries with his spirit." But Paul went on to write, "He who speaks in a tongue edifies himself, but he who prophesies edifies the church" (14:4).

The idea of speaking in tongues intrigued Ron but after various attempts at this type of prayer his fascination began to wane. He remembers praying in the privacy of his room in what sounded to his untrained ear like an American Indian language and feeling like an idiot. However, after all but giving up, another resident encouraged him to continue. Not long after that, something occurred that has never happened again. Praying rhythmically one night in an unrecognized cadence, a cleansing burst suddenly exploded in his gut. It reminded him of a mouth-cleansing burst of Binaca breath spray; it was as though his belly had been completely cleansed; an immediate impression of well-being stayed with him for several minutes. Obviously, the experience made a memorable impression; he couldn't help but believe he had been touched by the Holy Spirit. However, after a few more attempts to pray in tongues with no indication of any more belly-bursting sprays, he stopped. He became uncomfortable, not sure he deserved to be that close to what seemed to be a spiritual experience.

A volunteer teacher in his early fifties who lived in the nearby community took Ron under his wing. He taught Bible classes on certain daily visits during the week at the castle. As a pastor, he had studied Hebrew and Greek, interpreting scripture based on those languages, and was an excellent teacher. He became a good friend and invited Ron to stay overnight at his home several times. They often played chess and talked about issues of the day. His wife was always welcoming and provided good home cooking. A spiritual man, he never forced his opinions or religious philosophy on Ron in their discussions. In the short time they knew one another he became the most influential man in Ron's life except for his father.

Everyone in Teen Challenge insisted Christ could help Ron, and over the next six years his life became more stable. He graduated the program in early 1980, and a Teen Challenge director asked him to work as a bookkeeper in their office in Orange, California. He was required to track donations to the organization and record all expenditures; he was provided a minimal income—working paycheck to paycheck again—and a furnished room in the same building adjacent to the office. The entire year his focus was on mastering his work responsibilities and attending worship services conducted by the Teen Challenge pastor at Orange. Later on, he established a new accounting system for the office and for a minister's church in Lone Pine, California. Not much national news infiltrated his world during this time except for the Mount Saint Helens eruption in May and the November election of Ronald Reagan as president. Ron cast his vote for Jimmy Carter.

After about a year, an opportunity presented itself for him to move into a home with some fellow Teen Challenge graduates in the nearby city of Garden Grove. The ranch-style home shared with three other men had a kidney shaped pool in which his attempts to teach himself to swim proved marginally successful. His swimming abilities were limited to floating and dog paddling, but to some degree he had overcome a fear of the water. A former Peace Corps volunteer, who had to remind him of her visit, joined him at a worship service at Orange County Teen Challenge and a later visit to Disneyland. Three weekend getaways the following year are memorable: one weekend he and his housemates drove to the southern rim of the Grand Canyon. As the canyon became visible, its awesome expanse was just as breathtaking as the first time he stopped there eight years earlier. He and his friends hiked a trail into the canyon toward a point overlooking the Colorado River. Ron remembers it as being an excruciatingly painful experience because the hiking boots he wore were a poor fit. He didn't make it to the overlook but had to stop at a rest station at the bottom of the trail. By the time he crawled back to the top of the South Rim, his feet were blistered and bruised.

On another weekend, they drove to Palm Springs and watched a Cleveland Indians spring training game. It was fun to sit so close to the action and hear the crack of the bat on the ball. He went on a retreat for several days early that year with a group of people from Orange Teen Challenge. They drove south from the Salton Sea into northern Mexico to a hacienda owned by a friend of the pastor and stayed several days, long enough for Ron and the wife of the pastor to hike a nearby mountain range. The day before their return Ron thought someone from behind him was shaking the lounge chair he sat in, causing it to skitter across the cement floor porch. But no one was near him, and everyone else got shook up too, realizing a small earthquake had occurred, probably some distance away. One summer Ron found time to volunteer at a camp for kids near Big Bear Lake, but remembers more about the location than the children.

The release of the Iranian hostages on the day Reagan was sworn in as president preceded an assassination attempt a few months later. It came close to ending the president's life but at the time very few realized the seriousness of the wound. A milestone in the nation's history occurred in September: Reagan's nominee to the Supreme Court, Sandra Day O'Conner, was confirmed as associate justice, the first woman appointed to the highest court in the country. Five other justices had been appointed since the confirmation of Thurgood Marshall, including Chief Justice William Rehnquist in 1971, a Nixon nominee.

Ron began to look for a new job near the end of the year; earnings and a general dissatisfaction with the work at Teen Challenge prompted his search. He scoured employment advertisements and a position working for the city of Anaheim posted in the local newspaper caught his eye. He applied for the job, and in May 1982 was hired to work as a clerk in their maintenance division. Soon after beginning employment, Ron was called for jury duty, a process that required him to appear on several court days and stand by for the random selection process. Since he had just started his new job, he was not looking forward to being seated. As luck would have it, he was the first person selected to serve on the Hillside Strangler jury. At the request of his supervisor with the city, he asked the judge to be released from that jury. The judge seemed to view his request unfavorably and Ron waited in the jury box most of the rest of the day while other selected jurors were seated. Just when it looked like the trial was to begin, the judge turned his attention back to Ron and asked him if he still wanted to appeal his juror service. When

Ron answered in the affirmative, he was excused from the jury and avoided serving on what turned out to be the longest criminal trial case in United States history at the time, lasting two years.

Not long before starting to work with the city, a bald tire caused his motorcycle to skid on a highway entrance ramp; fortunately, a trailing car swerved to avoid him but after the accident he decided to sell the motorcycle. He had already sold the TR-3 sportscar. He purchased a moped—he thinks it was a Vespa—and it became his mode of transportation from Garden Grove to his job, which was an adventure in itself. Work with the city soon became routine. A few of his summer evenings were spent in Anaheim's central park enjoying outdoor classic feature films. The movies, along with an appreciation of Don's study at the American Film Institute, began to raise his interest in films; collecting a catalog of classic and current movies later formed his DVD library.

Ron's minimal efforts to engage in social activities failed. He enjoyed a Sunday evening Bible study at Calvary Church in Costa Mesa because the pastor read from the scriptures word for word, with his comments interspersed here and there. He thought of a possible opportunity for female companionship at the study but it never happened; his financial and social insecurities continued to plague him and relationships with the people in the enormous study group, held in the main church foyer, never materialized. Interactions with the people he worked with were fine but his efforts to date the secretary at the Orange County Teen Challenge failed. She was an Armenian woman earnest in the appreciation of her ancestry. He became friends with a graduate of the women's Teen Challenge program but a relationship never blossomed. His three housemates at the Garden Grove home were considered friends and friendly, but all were related in some way to Teen Challenge and were not helpful in expanding his social interactions.

United States space shuttle flights progressed in the early eighties; in 1983 several technological innovations came to the forefront:

the protocol creating the internet was accepted; compact discs and players were sold for the first time in the United States; Bill Gates introduced the Windows operating system for the computer.

In the summer of 1984, the ceremonial torch of the Olympic Games was carried on the street past their Garden Grove home.

An Olympic torch runner on Garden Grove Boulevard, Garden Grove, California, in 1984

Later that year, while still searching for a new job, his father contacted him to say his mother had been diagnosed with breast cancer. Having formed no lasting relationships in California he decided to return to Ohio. It happened that she had a partial mastectomy and overcame the breast cancer. At the same time, it was discovered she had ovarian cancer, but a hysterectomy solved that issue too. She made a complete recovery before Ron quit his job with the city but he had already made up his mind to leave California and return to Ohio. His friend and teacher at Teen Challenge sold his 1976 Dodge Colt to him for a minimal price when he learned Ron wanted to return home by car.

Before leaving California, Ron used his last earned vacation days to visit Catalina Island. His planned return trip went north through Oregon and Washington before turning east. He drove through heavy snowfall on Washington's Snoqualmie Pass Interstate 90, and it continued to snow as far east as Montana but the roads were clear and the rest of his trip home was uneventful. Ron's future was up in the air again; no plans. Not long after his return, Ronald Reagan was reelected for a second term as president. Ron voted for him this time.

CHAPTER 7
1985-1990

His father put Ron to work through the spring and summer of 1985 trimming branches along a wooded section of his property; the branches bordering the field hung over portions of the crop area and hindered harvesting. It paid for Ron's room and board. At Teen Challenge he had studied Christianity different from his Lutheran upbringing and was reading the Bible daily. Unable or unwilling to form any close relationships, he entertained the thought of becoming a monk after reading the works of Thomas Merton, an American Trappist monk, member of the Abbey of Our Lady of Gethsemane in Bardstown, Kentucky. He even drove there and found the monastery, but apprehensions about embracing monastic dictates and fulfilling its decrees caused him to have second thoughts. However, the idea of a spiritual purpose for his life did not end in Bardstown. He traveled to Columbus occasionally and on those trips his attention was directed to the Methodist School of Theology campus in Delaware, Ohio. He visited the campus one day, but upon learning of his Lutheran baptism he was referred to Trinity Lutheran Seminary in Columbus. The seminary accepted him into its Christian education program in the fall of 1985, which was designed to lead him to a teaching position. He would soon realize his selected course of study would not be completed.

Antonin Scalia was confirmed to be an associate judge on the Supreme Court the following year, but several tragedies dominated the news including the loss of seven astronauts in the January explosion of the Space Shuttle Challenger, the Chernobyl disaster in April, and the Iran-Contra scandal near the end of the year. Ron's own personal tragedy took place after learning, to his surprise, that both men and women were enrolled at the seminary. He expected, and would have preferred, a male-only environment. However, his disappointment was tempered when a woman student studying to become a pastor caught his eye. They dated but their brief intimacy triggered another period of unrest for him. Sleepless nights and sporadic hallucinations similar to what he experienced years earlier raised their ugly heads again and the symptoms required a third trip to a hospital mental ward.

Ron has no memory of the approximate two week stay in the Riverside Hospital psychiatric unit, but the recuperative process included certain prescribed medications, Haldol being one. They were not effective. Psychiatric analysis was part of his recovery regimen for several months until those visits ended too. His recovery was slow; the relationship with the woman seminarian ended as did his enrollment at the seminary. His parents tried to be supportive but their main concern was with his sister still living at their home. He rented a room from a seminary professor and the next six months worked the phone lines for a county food pantry program. He also began attending a local church and was attracted to a woman congregant. She had no desire for a relationship but encouraged him to seek a job opening at The Ohio State University. In retrospect, he wondered if the Lord had brought them together because two short months after submitting his application the university called, and after a perfunctory interview, offered him a clerical job. He started the new job in September 1986 at Jones Tower, the former residence of the girl he briefly dated after he was discharged from the army. The tower was still providing housing for graduate students. A move to an off-campus apartment followed, and at age thirty-nine, The Ohio State University was going to provide his first retirement and health benefit package. Before starting the new job, Ron drove his Dodge Colt to Florida and stayed with a cousin and his wife near Orlando for two days before going on to Everglades National Park and an overnight stay in his car. The Everglades was interesting and he enjoyed the visit until he opened the car window and the interior became inundated with hordes of mosquitoes, which proceeded to bite him mercilessly.

The clerical position at Jones Graduate Tower included his first complete introduction to computer programs and their many database systems; his previous job at the food pantry called for only minimal computer familiarization. Ron was responsible for collecting rent payments in the last week of each month from the tower residents after which the payments were entered into a database file. Although he was nervous at first about working with credit card payments, it didn't take him long to catch on to the process; the computer work proved to be enjoyable too. In his spare time Ron experimented with different programs, and on one occasion inadvertently wiped clean all the stored data on the computer hard drive; the so-called formatting of the hard drive disk meant all the accounting records and operating system files were lost. However, his computer instructions included a backup procedure to record on an external storage disk all the receipted data; everything was recovered with the assistance and expertise of a university programmer. It taught him a valuable lesson he applied after purchasing his own home computer.

Intense political division took place near the end of 1987 when Robert Bork became a controversial Reagan nominee to fill a Supreme Court vacancy; his confirmation was defeated in the Senate. The following February, Anthony Kennedy was chosen to fill the vacancy and approved by the Senate.

Ron went on his first vacation while working at Ohio State the month before Kennedy was sworn in as Supreme Court justice. He flew to California to visit Don at his Glendale apartment. He returned home after a couple of weeks and continued to work at Jones Tower for another year until he was promoted to a clerk II position working at Mershon Auditorium. During this time his apartment was burglarized twice and a new place to live became a priority. In September 1988 he took the bold step of buying a house—a two-story home built in 1910—in Clintonville, a community in Columbus near the Ohio State campus.

Ron's home, circa 1990

As with his previous apartment, the house was a short one-mile bicycle ride to and from the campus but located in a less crime-ridden area. The home was reasonably priced at $36,000, but because of his financial situation he had to rely on the GI Bill. It offered a down payment for certain qualified housing for first-time home buyers and the purchase was approved. In earlier searches in the communities of German Village and Victorian Village, properties were listed as available for sale but the sellers would not accept a GI down payment authorization. His new home was on a block dominated by student rental properties, but two adjacent houses were private residences as was a home across the street. According to the property abstract of title, the 40-by-100-foot lot on which the house rested was originally part of a military tract of land granted to an individual by an act of Congress signed by then President John Adams in 1800, prior to Ohio statehood. He looked at the home twice before deciding it was right for him. The interior of the house was limited to four rooms—two upstairs and two downstairs plus a kitchen and an upstairs bathroom. Except for the kitchen and bathroom, all the floors were hardwood. Ceiling fans were located in the large upstairs bedroom and in the downstairs front room. A large low-clearance undeveloped cellar, best designed for a person with a maximum height of five-foot-six and not his five-foot-eleven frame, had three large rooms. Its cement floor could not be confused with a furnished, stylish basement. There was a basic shower, commode, and gas-fired water heater and boiler. As far as Ron was concerned, the boiler was the unique feature of the home; hot water was pumped through the house into cast iron radiators that heated the rooms. He had never lived in a home with radiated heat, but his concerns were unfounded as the hot water heating proved to be very efficient. His purchase of a washing machine and dryer completed the basement furnishings.

    Ron encouraged his parents to attend a seminar at Ohio State about family members with a mental illness. The seminar seemed to remove some of the stigma they carried concerning his sister's condition and suggested they could secure Medicaid funding so his sister could live in a nursing home in Bucyrus. She had lived with their parents twenty years and with Medicaid funding they were able to place her in a full-time care facility that included a work program for the disabled designed to keep her active and energized, something his parents were no longer able to do. In October, Ron drove his parents in their car on a vacation, going to Niagara Falls before stopping in Cooperstown, New York, to visit the Baseball Hall of Fame. From there a drive through the New England states and on into New York City followed before concluding the trip with a stop in Harrisburg, Pennsylvania, to visit the

Hershey chocolate factory. After returning home, the presidential elections took place; Ron voted for George H.W. Bush, who was elected president, handily defeating his Democratic rival, Michael Dukakis. Bush had served eight years as vice president for Reagan and had extensive prior political experience.

The year 1989 had some traumatic events and a remarkable development. In March, the Exxon-Valdez oil tanker spill in Alaska's Prince William Sound is considered the worst in terms of damage to the environment. Beginning in April, the Tiananmen Square protests reflected economic and social change being called for in China. The protests were finally quelled in June by the use of military force. The twenty-five-year Wynford High School class reunion was held in July. Don returned from California and accompanied Ron to the reunion; it was disappointing for Ron. Some former classmates he looked forward to seeing did not attend, and several others did not seem to be interested to renew old acquaintances. In October, a year after their New England tour, Ron took his parents on another east coast trip, visiting Washington, DC, and driving through Virginia with stops at Mount Vernon, Monticello, and the presidential homes of Madison and Monroe. Soon after returning from their trip, the Iron Curtain came down; the amazing fall of the Berlin Wall in November led to the reunification of Germany the next year and the end of the Cold War.

Ohio State posted a new position for accountant with the Physics Department in 1990, and Ron's application was accepted. The job consisted of maintaining purchase and expense ledgers for the professors and instructors. His employment coincided with the appointment of a woman manager to replace the current retiring supervisor; they had a good working relationship for a while. Keith, a friend over the years, began work in the physics office sometime later. After a second promotion at Ohio State, a celebration was in order. Ron sold the Dodge Colt that was nearing the end of its effective life and made his first new car purchase, a Geo Metro. It turned out to be a fine investment. Considered a town car, its main selling point was an excellent fifty-mile per gallon of gasoline fuel consumption. The car was surprisingly roomy and comfortable to drive. It had plenty of space to carry his bicycle to eight different thirty-mile bicycle loop rides in and around central Ohio in late summer.

Two events gained attention that year. Nelson Mandela was released from a South African jail after serving twenty-seven years as a political prisoner and later served as president of South Africa. Also, near the end of summer, Iraq invaded neighboring Kuwait to begin the short-lived Gulf War; Iraqi forces were routed when the United States came to the rescue of Kuwait early the next year.

CHAPTER 8
1991-1994

Ron joined his parents celebrating their fiftieth wedding anniversary in 1991. In the summer, he drove them in their car on an ambitious vacation to the western states of Colorado, New Mexico, Arizona, Utah, Wyoming, and South Dakota, stopping first in Springfield, Missouri, where his father had served in the army. The hospital he worked in for over three years had been torn down. They continued on to Colorado. Ron drove to the top of Pikes Peak in an exhilarating drive both going up and coming back down. Then they visited the Garden of the Gods national landmark near Colorado Springs. Carlsbad Caverns in New Mexico was next on their itinerary followed by a stop at the south rim of the Grand Canyon in Arizona, reminding Ron of his two other visits there; it was still awe-inspiring. From the canyon he drove through the Painted Desert and Monument Valley in Arizona and on to Zion National Park in Utah before they were welcomed to Afton, Wyoming, by the world's largest elk antler arch spanning a downtown street. On a short hike Ron and his mother encountered a young moose munching leaves from a fallen tree beside their path but it didn't seem to be bothered by them. From Afton, Ron drove on into Yellowstone National Park where scarred trees from a devastating fire several years before were still evident; the damaged trees did not detract from the beauty of the other park landscapes or the rush of the Old Faithful geyser. After a brief stop at Jackson Hole at the base of Grand Teton National Park, they continued on through the Badlands of South Dakota and a visit to Mount

Rushmore before heading east and a return to Ohio, logging 5,750 miles. Ron thought his father enjoyed this trip much more than their previous East Coast tours.

In July, President Bush nominated Clarence Thomas to succeed retiring Supreme Court Justice Thurgood Marshall. After a contentious hearing, Thomas was confirmed in October.

The next year Ron went on a solo vacation drive to Charleston, South Carolina, stopping on the way at the site of his basic training days at Fort Jackson. After an over twenty-year interval, the layout of the fort did not look familiar to him and stirred up no old memories. He enjoyed Charleston, visits to Fort Sumter and a nearby plantation. On his return to Ohio, he stopped at Myrtle Beach for a couple of days but thought it would have been more enjoyable if someone had accompanied him. Two years of cordiality between the woman manager and Ron at Ohio State's Physics Department had begun to deteriorate by the end of 1992; tensions had surfaced between them and his job gave him no opportunity for advancement or promotion. So, after six years at Ohio State, he applied for, and was awarded, a position with the state of Ohio; the move provided upward mobility and allowed him to continue to meet home mortgage payments; he still lived paycheck-to-paycheck.

Other events in 1992: Johnny Carson retired after 30 years on the Tonight Show; an arms reduction agreement between the United States and the newly named country of Russia was signed; William Jefferson Clinton defeated George H.W. Bush in the election for president in November, Ron voted for the independent candidate Ross Perot. Later that month, IBM introduced the first smart phone, the IBM Simon.

When Ron joined the state of Ohio to begin work in January 1993 his retirement and health benefits were not interrupted because both The Ohio State University and the state shared a common benefit package through the Ohio Public Employees Retirement Benefits System. His vacation and sick leave balances from Ohio State also were transferred to the state. His new job was as an account examiner in the Department of MRDD (mentally retarded and developmentally disabled—later to become the Department of Developmental Disabilities). Almost from the start, he became attracted to an African American woman co-worker. His attraction to her plus the stress of a new job prompted another set of sleepless nights until prolonged fatigue required him to seek medical attention. Someone referred him to a psychiatrist—a third important male figure in his life. Because of Ron's distraught, exhausted condition at their first meeting, the psychiatrist admitted Ron to the Mount Carmel hospital psychiatric ward. He prescribed Lithium medication for a bipolar episode. His diagnosis of an illness helped Ron understand the cause of his four hospitalizations, and the subsequent successful use of the Lithium over the next twenty-five years proved it was treatable. He discussed with the psychiatrist a theory that the LSD he had taken in the army may have contributed to bipolar incidences. The psychiatrist said he could give him no definitive answer because few studies had been conducted to verify or disprove that assertion. He went on to say risk factors with LSD ingredients could be a "stressor," meaning a reaction such as those Ron had experienced could be possible associated with stress.

Ron came upon a Bible verse in the book of Acts attributed to Paul and Barnabas. They said, "We must go through many hardships to enter the Kingdom of God" (14:22). Of course, Paul was surely referring to his being stoned because he had preached the good news of what God had done for the Jews and Gentiles in the region of Turkey: the good news being, "For God so loved the world that he gave his one and only Son, that whoever believes in him shall not perish but have eternal life" (John 3:16); he was proclaiming the mystery of Christ. Ron knew the oft-quoted verse in John but he didn't know how to trust in God. He confidently relied on his parents in his youth and took for granted a love for them, but as an adult the only person he could say he loved, sadly, was himself. And there were times he didn't love himself either. After his first and subsequent hospitalizations he had trusted very few people.

He believed in other accounts of historical people and events. The signing of the Magna Carta in 1215 is well-documented; Napoleon's wars in Europe have been chronicled; events in America in the eighteenth and nineteenth centuries—the Declaration of Independence and the Civil War—are recorded for posterity; stories of past presidents including Washington, Jefferson, and Lincoln are readily accepted as fact, though none of us living today were witnesses to those people or proceedings. Ron tried to understand why the ancient texts of the Bible did not carry the same weight for him as stories of many other historical events and people. Understanding them was difficult for him because, belonging to the very distant past, the gospels and writings of Paul and the apostles portray accounts of Jesus that seem more mysterious than historical. But he could not deny the spread of Christianity as recorded by history after the death and crucifixion of Jesus.

Ron's health benefits paid most of his hospital bills for a two week stay at Mount Carmel. His previous hospital bills, minimal compared to current costs, had all been paid from saved earnings. Sick leave balances transferred from Ohio State were used for his loss of days at the state. Unlike previous hospitalizations, he was able to return to work and continue a normal lifestyle. He continued to use Lithium daily and had periodic, routine visits with the psychiatrist.

Largely overlooked because of his stay in the hospital was the attempt to bomb the World Trade Center in New York in February. Other national and world events went unnoticed too. For example, the formal establishment of the European Union. In June, Ron's Aunt Mary, the wife of his Uncle Warren, his father's next oldest brother, died of cancer at the early age of 55. Uncle Warren was an avid bowler and he and Aunt Mary met at a bowling alley when he was thirty-nine. Ron thinks there was a seventeen-year difference in their ages and had heard his mother say he would never marry, but she was wrong. He and Aunt Mary had two children and were married thirty-two years.

A lot of Ron's time during the year was devoted to learning the ins and outs of horse racing. Jeff, his new boss at MR/DD, was a thoroughbred horse racing enthusiast and piqued his interest in the sport by giving him introductory literature and explaining the ways to bet. Together, they visited Ohio race tracks in Columbus, Cincinnati, and Cleveland between fifteen and twenty times in 1993. Although his effort to develop an intimate relationship with the African- American woman failed, they enjoyed a platonic rapport and spent many evenings together.

In August, President Clinton's nominee for justice of the Supreme Court, Ruth Bader Ginsberg, was confirmed with remarkably little dissent.

In January 1994, his vacation visit to Don in California came soon after the Northridge earthquake, and a few evidences of damage near his Glendale apartment were obvious. Ron twice went to watch the horse races at the Santa Anita thoroughbred track in Arcadia. In June, the astonishing news that O.J. Simpson may have murdered his ex-wife and a friend began to dominate the headlines. Later that year Ron decided to trade in his Geo Metro and signed a three-year lease on a new Nissan Sentra. On a long weekend by himself in Chicago, he attended a Cubs baseball game at Wrigley Field and watched thoroughbred horses race at the Arlington Park in Arlington Heights. His psychiatrist, who had encouraged him to think about ending the relationship with the African American woman, correctly surmised there was no future for them as a couple. Before breaking up, they toured the Smoky Mountains together on an August weekend, driving on a portion of the Bluegrass Parkway. The month before their weekend together Stephen Breyer, another Clinton nominee to the Supreme Court, was confirmed.

CHAPTER 9
1995-2000

Ron decided to search for a new partner at the end of August. Social media was not a source of connecting with people at the time so at the age of forty-seven, and no longer frequenting churches or bars, he decided on a time-honored practice and placed an ad in the personal column of the Columbus paper: Male seeking female who is honest, practical, and affectionate.

Several women responded to the advertisement. The first two women Ron met for dinner were pleasant enough, but he was not attracted to them and didn't attempt a follow-up meeting. The second woman he met confronted him at the end of their meal saying, in an annoyed tone, "You're not going to call me again, are you?" When Ron watched the movie *Sea of Love* a few years later he remembered the woman's response because in the film, Detective Al Pacino tries to get fingerprints on a glass from a lady he meets on a blind date. Not realizing his motive, she confronts him in the same way in the same tone of voice as the woman Ron met.

He met the third woman at Frisch's Big Boy on the west side of town near her home. Judy reminded him of Annie in the movie of the same name; she had curly red hair with rosy cheeks and a young woman's body even though she was Ron's age. Raised in Fredericktown, a small town in northern Ohio, she graduated from Otterbein University the same year he graduated from Kent, and was working as an analyst for an insurance company near downtown Columbus. She was passionate but otherwise had a very quiet, gentle spirit; she was not a conversationalist. However, she revealed a previous five-year marriage had ended in divorce quite a few years earlier and a longer relationship had ended several months prior to their first date. After several dates, he decided it was only fair to tell her about his hospitalizations.

Together over a year, he decided parting company and going their separate ways was the sensible thing to do. From his point of view, they were not communicating effectively. His plan adhered to another time-honored practice: meet her for lunch and explain his point of view, but his attempt to end the relationship failed. He was caught off guard when she burst into tears, to the dismay of several other diners.

He began to have second thoughts about a breakup; nearing the age of fifty it was likely his life would return to its former lonely existence. That night he apologized over the phone and asked her to consider continuing the relationship. She talked with her sister and afterwards agreed to give it another try; over many more years their relationship has grown; a mutual respect, accepting each other for who they are, has kept them together. Judy has been a stabilizing person in his life. No doubt her partnership, the proper medication for his bipolar condition, and the understanding that God is faithful (Lamentations 3:22-23) helped eliminate any future hospitalizations for the mental illness. He has thanked God for the medications and for bringing Judy into his life.

Judy's love of travel equaled his fanaticism for Cleveland Indians baseball. Before they met, she had gone on several cruises with a female co-worker and the travel bug had bitten her bad. Little did Ron know their future together would include tours all over the world. In their first year together their travel was limited to weekend trips or vacations to Cincinnati, Cleveland, Chicago, and Pittsburgh.

Early in 1995, O.J. Simpson was acquitted in the murder trial that began the previous year. The April bombing of the Oklahoma Federal Building was a national calamity; it took 168 lives. In October, the Cleveland Indians appeared in their first World Series since

1954 but lost in six games to the Atlanta Braves. When the Browns of Cleveland left for Baltimore at the end of the year, Ron's taste for pro football soured as player salaries soared.

The next year, he and Judy continued their travels, going on trips to Florida, Las Vegas, and Canada. Then in June, the unexpected happened. Ron's mother, aged seventy-eight, was killed in an automobile accident. Two months later, his father died of a heart condition at the age of seventy-five, probably hastened by his mother's death. Ron's sister was a passenger in the car accident that killed their mother but was not seriously injured. The accident confirmed Ron's understanding of the tormenting disease that plagued his sister; when notified their mother had died in the accident, she showed little emotion even though, as an occupant in the car, she could have realized what happened. He said it was as if she was completely detached from the tragedy, but maybe that was good.

After his parents died, he began to commute regularly between Columbus and Bucyrus to visit her; they would go for a meal or just ride around. She seemed to welcome Ron's visits, especially when he stopped to get them an ice cream treat.

In November, Bill Clinton was reelected president, winning a second term over his main competitor, Bob Dole. Ron voted for the electors of Harry Browne and Art Olivier, presidential and vice-presidential candidates of the Libertarian Party. At the end of the year, he and Judy drove to Savannah, Georgia, to relax for a few days. It had been a difficult year.

In the first months of 1997, Judy and Ron traveled to Kentucky and New York. Much of the news that year focused on two events: O.J. Simpson was found liable in a civil suit brought by the families for the wrongful deaths of the victims in the previous criminal case. Attracting even more attention was the death of Diana, Princess of Wales, in a car accident in Paris. The three-year lease on Ron's Nissan Sentra expired in the summer and he signed another three-year Nissan lease. His attention on the World Series in October between the Indians and Miami Marlins ended in frustration as once again the Tribe lost in seven games, the seventh game ending in extra innings.

Ron and Judy began the next year with a memorable vacation to Texas with stops in San Antonio, Big Bend National Park, and Corpus Christi.

Judy in Big Bend National Park, Texas, at Rio Grande River in 1998

In April, Ron auctioned the debt-free farm home his parents willed to him. Also, a wrongful death suit against the family of the driver who caused the accident that killed his mother was settled. His father had initiated the suit before his death. Ron invested the money from these actions in the stock market, in securities he thought might have been favored by his parents; he selected farm-related and educational stocks. For the first time, Ron's paycheck-to-paycheck lifestyle was backed by investments, compliments of his parents. The market value of the investments grew exponentially, enduring the dot-com bubble burst, 9/11, and the stock market swoon caused by the bank bailout. He and

Judy vacationed in Boston in July. In October they enjoyed a live stage performance by John and June Carter Cash. At the end of the year, Ron had his house sided with vinyl and his porches and gutters repaired.

The year 1999 was only a couple of weeks old when Ron and Judy headed south to stay for eight days at Fort Myers Beach, Florida. It was one of their better vacations up to that time as far as being able to relax; the nice weather helped. The last two days in Clearwater Beach the temperature was over eighty degrees and about ten degrees above normal for the entire trip. Relaxing on the beach, hiking in a nature preserve, riding a swamp cruiser, and a visit to the home of Thomas Edison filled some of their days. Ron even won money at the thoroughbred racetrack in Tampa. After returning from Florida, Ron celebrated his birthday by purchasing his first new computer: a Micron Desk Top. The computer with printer cost just over $2,000 and the internet connection was about thirty dollars per month. Interestingly, many hardware costs have since gone down while charges by service providers seem to be on the rise. The ability to communicate by email, access the internet to do banking, track investments, and shop online made for what he thought was a good investment. The option to play games never appealed to him that much, although a computer chess partner proved to be challenging.

In February, President Clinton was acquitted of a House of Representatives' impeachment by a trial in the Senate. That same month Ron accepted a new position with Ohio MR/DD. After six years reviewing client records as an account examiner in the Division of Resource and Liability, he was promoted to management analyst in a recently redefined Office of Medicaid Payments and Support. The job involved approving pay authorizations to home care providers and to other people contributing assistance to the waiver support programs. To put it more simply, he reviewed a coworker's data before performing his own routine data entry to finalize the pay authorization process. It was an easy, if not satisfying, job; the people with whom he worked were pleasant and worked hard including his new woman supervisor. They got along much better than his previous female manager at Ohio State.

In March, Don returned from California and decided to stay in Ohio for several more months, shuttling back and forth between Ron's home and his parents' home. Ron's spring project was screening the back porch to allow a bug-free environment and Don was a big help when he began the job in April. The work on the small porch went fast. Once it was planned, it took just a few days to buy the material, put up the framing and complete the screening. The lowest quote from a contractor to do the job had been $1,500. The material, including a new exterior screen door, cost $250. The labor was certainly less than $1,250, and they had the satisfaction of having completed the job themselves. About the time the project was finished the shocking news of the Columbine High School shooting in Colorado was reported. Thirteen students were killed and more than that number were injured.

In May, Ron tackled a second project: repairing the roof on the old garage. Several rows of roofing material, roof cement and some roofing nails were required. Of course, the job turned out to be more difficult than it appeared. Don showed up when the project was almost finished but provided needed help. Ron and Judy decided to travel to Chester, West Virginia, for a vacation weekend. Chester, across the Ohio River from East Liverpool, Ohio, is the home to Mountaineer Racetrack. Ron said much better options than a weekend at a thoroughbred racetrack could be found, but conditioned that opinion, adding winning a few bets might factor into the decision.

Ron traveled with Keith, his former co-worker at Ohio State, to Cincinnati and Cleveland to watch the Reds and the Tribe play each other several times that summer. At the end of June, Ron watched Diana Krall perform at the Jazz and Rib Festival in downtown Columbus. He and Judy attended a Tony Bennett concert several years earlier. Diana Krall was good too, performing on an outdoor stage. In August, Ron and Judy went on a vacation to Canada, stopping first at Sarasota Springs, New York, to watch the thoroughbreds. After stopping one night in Ticonderoga, New York, they drove on to Quebec City and Montreal in Quebec, and finally to Ottawa, Ontario. It was an interesting trip. The highlight was probably the Chateau Frontenac—a historical 640-room hotel in Quebec City. Passing on a visit to the Notre Dame Cathedral in Montreal because it was under repair, their itinerary was changed to allow them to stop at a Montreal Expos baseball game against Cincinnati in Olympic Stadium. Returning to Ohio by way of Buffalo, New York, they stopped at Niagara Falls to see the falls lit up at night.

Judy passed a work anniversary in the year 2000 at her place of employment but was expecting to be laid off the next year. Her plan to retire on her birthday in 2002 had to be moved up. Once her employment ended, she wanted to sell her home, buy a condo or get an apartment, and travel. The millennium bug—the Y2K scare—ushered in the new century; concern about corporate profit declines due to lost computer data was the issue. Contrary to expectations, few major problems occurred because many programmers and computer information technology experts short-circuited the predicted glitches.

Ron had been thinking of terminating his employment at age fifty-five in 2002. His work with the pay authorization process for home-based individuals and agencies had become routine; the job no longer provided him with a sense of fulfillment. Except for past mental issues and a sinus condition, his health had been very good for most of his life but things started to change; he did not feel well for much of the rest of the year.

Ron's work began to suffer due to, among other things, high blood pressure. His vision became distorted at work one day; he had trouble focusing on the pay authorizations and didn't feel well so he went to the building nursing station. The nurse mistakenly recorded his blood pressure at 200/0 and encouraged him to seek medical attention and a doctor's diagnosis. A referral to a doctor confirmed high blood pressure but not the low diastolic pressure that had prompted the referral. Thus Ron began his journey through the maze of medications prescribed at different times over the years for blood pressure, high cholesterol, acid reflux, enlarged prostrate, neuropathy, and celiac disease. His personal care physicians supplemented their expertise, referring him over time to doctors specializing in nephrology, orthopedics, gastroenterology, cardiology, urology, dermatology, and allergies. His bipolar diagnosis required him to have his Lithium medication managed by a psychiatrist. Health issues caused him to rethink future plans; he temporarily put on hold thoughts of early retirement because benefits provided by the state would cover many of the now higher costs of health care.

In January, before his health scare, he and Judy headed south to vacation for eight days in Florida, staying in Fort Lauderdale two nights, at the Bay Breeze Hotel in Key Largo several nights, and returning to Miami Beach for their last two nights. The temperature was always in the mid-seventies range. Walking tours, a visit to Wolfie's Restaurant in South Miami Beach, and a stop at Gulfstream Park on their last day occupied some of their time. In February, Don returned from California and stayed in Ohio until July, shuttling back and forth between Ron's home and his parents' home. He and Ron got together occasionally during those few months.

Ron's Uncle John, the husband of his father's only sister, died in March. Ron never had that close of a relationship with him, but recalled him being a genuinely positive, happy person. He always treated Ron as an individual. He remembered as a teenager Uncle John talking to him in an inclusive way, as an adult, one summer day at the Farm Bureau. His father and Uncle John were in the midst of a conversation when his father was called away. His uncle turned to him and asked him how he was doing and engaged him in a conversation. He was not being polite; he wanted feedback, asking for Ron's opinions.

The collapse of the dotcom bubble began in the year 2000 due to excessive speculation of internet companies from 1995 to

2000, when the NASDAQ exchange rose over 400 percent. From March 2000 to 2002, the exchange fell 78% signaling the end of an investment craze directed toward those companies. The investments Ron made had not gone to internet or tech companies so his market losses were negligible. In fact, his investment funds grew even after the purchase of a new Chrysler PT Cruiser; his second Nissan Sentra lease expired in June. A few months later he hired a contractor to renovate his home; a wall was removed to make a more spacious living room. Of course, the job turned out to be more difficult than it appeared, and instead of taking nine days as initially estimated the project took well over a month. The fact the house was messed up for so long may have contributed to his missing several work days due to hypertension. Blood pressure medication that had been discontinued at the end of last year was prescribed again by his doctor.

Just like the previous year, he and Keith traveled to Cincinnati and Cleveland to watch the Reds and the Tribe in May, June, and July. Don returned to Ohio early in the year by car, driving a northerly route, and had already decided he wanted to return to California in a few months by way of the Gulf Coast. Ron took a vacation week in mid-July to go with him as far as New Orleans, stopping briefly at the casinos in Biloxi, but the real story was the intense heat. Fine beaches in Mississippi had no sunbathers because it was so hot. After a couple of nights in New Orleans, Don took Ron to Jackson, Mississippi, and a flight back to Ohio, and Don continued on to California.

At the end of August, Ron and Judy went on a vacation to San Diego. It was an opportunity for Ron to revisit the city after a twenty-year absence. Their home base for the next week became The Lafayette Hotel Swim Club and Bungalows (known at that time as Inn Suites Hotel) on El Cajon Boulevard located within a mile or so of the San Diego Zoo and Balboa Park. The hotel was fine. Under apparent new ownership it is advertised as an iconic San Diego boutique hotel. Supposedly many movie stars stayed there in the forties and fifties. Their room was the Ingrid Bergman suite; it was small but clean and well maintained. They enjoyed a buffet breakfast every day, and the famed Johnny Weissmuller Olympic Pool was available. A rented car allowed them to visit several places each day. The Hotel Del Coronado and beaches on Coronado Island was one of their first stops.

Hotel del Coronado, Coronado, California

They went to a different destination almost every day: the zoo, Balboa Park, the ocean beach communities, and downtown San Diego; La Jolla to examine the tide pools at several beaches, and the thoroughbred races at Del Mar. On yet another day, they drove to Anaheim late one afternoon to take in a baseball game. Their eighth and last night, they were surprised by a visit from Don. They had made arrangements to meet him in Anaheim, but never connected so he stopped to see them on his way to Phoenix.

In November, one of the closest presidential elections in United States history took place. Texas Governor George W. Bush lost the popular vote to Vice President Al Gore but gained the required electoral votes by a slim margin. Controversy over ballots cast in the state of Florida ultimately led to a Supreme Court decision confirming the results and ended any recounts with Bush leading by 537 votes. Ron cast his vote for Bush.

In early December, Judy was terminated by her employer after twenty-three years. Notified earlier of her pending termination, she continued to work with the insurance carrier as part of a transition team, agreeing to work because it paid her a higher severance package but she fell fourteen months short of a retirement goal that would have provided her with a health benefit. Ron continued to work as a management analyst for the state of Ohio, but his job was changed. The new position with the state required comparative cost analysis and was more challenging. He continued to have health problems and relied on his health benefits to pay most of the doctor bills. Rethinking his early retirement had been carefully considered and turned out to be a wise decision. His sister continued to live at the nursing facility in Bucyrus and participate in a work program three days each week. She seemed to appreciate the food and activities available and was able to attend several events during the year.

CHAPTER 10
2001-2004

Ron and Judy traveled Florida in February 2001. They stayed one week at the Clearwater Beach Palm Pavilion Inn, visiting Sarasota's Ringling Brothers Circus Museum, a Siesta Key beach, Venice Beach, and Tarpon Springs, one of the sponge capitals of the world. They dined at the Columbia Restaurant in Tampa's trendy Ibor City one night too. The weather was warm, not hot, and the water was cold. It was a relaxing, enjoyable week, but the next months were distressing. In April, Judy's father died suddenly at the age of eighty-one. He had worked as a machinist during most of his life and cared diligently for his wife in his retirement. She died in October at age eighty-three after having suffered with Alzheimer's disease for several years. It was a very tough time for Judy and her sister. Between the dates of their parents' deaths, the country experienced its own distressing time because of the heinous attack of 9/11 on the twin towers in New York. The aftermath of that event led to the war in Afghanistan the following month and it lasted twenty years.

Over the Thanksgiving holiday Ron and Judy decided to drive south to the Gulf Coast and eventually reached New Orleans. After driving to Memphis, Tennessee, the first night, they took a more leisurely route the next day to Vicksburg, Mississippi, stopping at several river casinos. The drive was notable to Ron for all the cotton fields in full bloom waiting to be harvested. They learned later the cotton was usually picked in September but had been delayed that year due to weather conditions. Vicksburg is on the Yazoo and

Mississippi rivers and the site of a major Civil War battlefield and many historic homes. After leaving Vicksburg, they followed the tree-lined Natchez Trace to Natchez, Mississippi. Natchez is situated on the bank of the Mississippi River too; a walking tour of the historic district and dinner along the river preceded a day tour of two of the many antebellum homes that remain in the town.

After leaving Natchez they drove to Saint Francisville, Louisiana, another historic town along the river most notable for the home and gardens of the Rosedown Plantation. The estate had an oak-lined lane; huge gardens on either side led to the refurbished home. An overnight stay in Baton Rouge preceded their drive to the west side of the Mississippi and a stop at two more plantations, Oak Alley and the Laura plantations. The Laura Plantation is a restored historic Creole homestead, the supposed place of origin of the fictional tales of Uncle Remus (Br'er Rabbit, Br'er Fox, et al.). From the plantations it was a short drive to New Orleans for a two-night stay; walking tours of the river, the French Quarter, the Garden District, and a cemetery tour near the French Quarter district occupied most of their time. The last day in New Orleans, Thanksgiving Day, they went to the Fair Grounds Race Course before driving to a hotel stop in Alabama. The next day, an all-day drive got them back to Columbus in the early evening. The PT Cruiser logged a very comfortable 2,152 riding miles.

The Enron bankruptcy scandal at the end of the year drew attention to accounting and corporate fraud. It was a mixture of bad culture, aggressive sales incentives, and accounting manipulations.

Ron was still thinking about retirement at the beginning of 2002. But he figured if the economy completely tanked, his termination with the state of Ohio, hopefully effective in two and one-half years, could be extended. He continued to work every day and was thankful no major health issues were a concern. His sister continued to live at the Bucyrus nursing facility and when he visited her, usually twice each month, they typically dined at a restaurant or fast-food location and drove around the community. Near the end of the year

Judy convinced Ron to go on a Caribbean cruise with her that was scheduled to leave near the end of February. It would be his first cruise and the first of many tours over the next fifteen years.

He knew Judy had been on cruises before they met but didn't realize how eager she was to set sail again, minus the sails. She took charge of all the arrangements, booking the flight and reserving an interior cabin for the voyage. They flew to Fort Lauderdale for a scheduled embarkation date on the Golden Princess, a Princess Lines ship with a 2,600-passenger capacity, that was destined for Saint Maarten, Saint Thomas, and Princess Cays, Princess's own large private beach on the island of Eleuthera in the Bahamas; it was a scheduled one-week cruise before returning to Fort Lauderdale. Judy was flabbergasted when we received an upgrade to an exterior, balcony stateroom; on all her previous cruises she had an interior cabin. It was a very pleasant voyage. Ron was delightfully impressed with the ship amenities and enjoyed the destinations; the food was great and the weather was mostly sunny with daytime highs averaging eighty-five degrees. The one time it rained the ship was between ports of call. The only brisk sea occurred returning to Florida on their last night before returning to Ohio.

With no extra vacation time, Ron was unable to join Judy on a tour of Spain in June. But in mid-August, he and Judy set out for Glacier National Park in northwest Montana. Their trip several years earlier to Big Bend National Park proved to be a surprisingly good time and the hope was a trip to the Northwest would be similarly fine. It was. Driving Ron's PT Cruiser, the route was planned well in advance, through Indiana, Illinois, Wisconsin, Minnesota, North Dakota, and finally Montana. On the way back, their route passed through Wyoming and South Dakota. The 4,820-mile trip included stops at quite a few places on the way before reaching Glacier National. At their first stop, Wisconsin's Dells, a ride on the Ducks, a land and water halftrack vehicle, carried them onto the Wisconsin River. They shopped in the Mall of America in Minneapolis and then continued west for a stop at both the north and south units of Theodore Roosevelt National Park in North Dakota, observing quite a few buffalo, some wild horses, a deer with her two young fawns, and lots of prairie dogs in their prairie dog towns.

Glacier National Park is a picturesque landscape of ice-covered mountains, lakes, flowers, and berries. Mountain peaks twelve thousand feet high with visible glaciers, though diminished in size recently, were covered at lower levels with pine forests and split by deep gorges. Before entering the park, Judy took over the wheel and drove twenty miles north of the Canadian border for a look at the Prince of Wales Hotel in Canada's Waterton Lakes National Park. Returning to Many Glaciers Lodge in Glacier National Park for a two-night stay, they went on a scenic boat tour on the lake next to the lodge and hiked several trails, taking care since it was bear season—sighting one bear at a great distance (other visitors had seen many bears). A Red Bus tour car took them over the one road that traverses the park; there were spectacular views and mountain goats and a big horn sheep was sighted near the roadway.

*Glacier National Park, Montana –
Paramount Pictures' mountain logo, back center*

Snow was still visible on the slopes and it was sweater weather at times, but the weather couldn't have been better. Many Glaciers Lodge was huge. The central lounge was big, yet cozily warm with two large fire places. The rooms were spacious and comfortable.

After two nights at the lodge they drove the only road through the park, the same road the Red Bus tour car had used, departing Glacier National on its western slope and headed south, arriving the second day at Yellowstone National Park. Both having seen Old Faithful and the Paint Pots in the southern part of the park on separate visits in the past, and since it was a free admission day with an expected big crowd, they decided not to go to those more famous sites. Instead, they stopped near the northwest entrance at Mammoth Springs, before proceeding to Norris Geyser, stopping briefly to watch a bear in the distance. Later, they enjoyed a picnic lunch at Virginia Falls; half a dozen large female elk passed them during their meal. On the way to Yellowstone Lodge and Yellowstone Lake, a large buffalo herd crossed their path. After exiting the northeast corner of the park, they drove over the wonderfully scenic eleven-thousand-foot Beartooth Pass and scared out several deer on the descent. They went on to visit the site of the Little Bighorn battlefield in Montana, Devil's Tower in Wyoming—the ambience around the tower was perceptible—and the South Dakota towns of Deadwood and Scenic—with all its cow skulls—near the Badlands. Their final stops were at Mount Rushmore, the city of Wall—famous for Wall Drug—and Mitchell, South Dakota, home of the Corn Palace. Judy had never been to any of the last locations and was particularly impressed with Mount Rushmore. After their return they went to several Ohio fall festivals and fairs.

In November, the United Nations voted to approve a disarmament plan for Iraq. In December, Judy applied for seasonal employment with Macy's and was hired at a store near her home.

In January 2003, Judy made all the arrangements for a vacation to Cancun and a room at the pyramid-shaped Hotel Camino Real surrounded by huge swimming pools. It was very relaxing. One day was set aside to visit the ruins at Chichen Itza.

The Chichen Itza pyramid on Yucatan Peninsula, Mexico, in 2003

The steep flight of steps on the pyramid made it difficult to ascend. Many people could not make it to the top. Ron decided to give it a try and made it with no problem only to discover his camera was with Judy. He climbed down and trudged back to the top to take some pictures. On another day they went into Cancun city to attend a bullfight, but Judy enjoyed, more than anything else, their day trip to the Isla Mujeres (Island of Women), stating the beaches were the best she had visited in all her travels.

On February 1, 2003, the Space Shuttle Columbia disaster occurred, disintegrating as it reentered Earth's atmosphere, killing all seven astronauts aboard. The Space Shuttle program was ended in 2011 and no further spacecraft were launched from American soil until the SpaceX 2020.

In April, Judy and her sister visited Las Vegas, the Grand Canyon, and other sites in Arizona. While they were on their trip, Ron went to Hot Springs, Arkansas, for a few days, stopping at Oaklawn Park thoroughbred racetrack on two different days, briefly touring Hot Springs National Park, and enjoyed a natural mineral spring bath. Judy and her sister went to Washington State and Oregon in June while Ron continued to work at his job with the state.

At the end of August, Judy booked them on their most ambitious vacation yet, a Mediterranean cruise starting from Venice aboard the same Golden Princess they toured the Caribbean on the previous year. Their luggage was lost by Air France but recovered shortly before the ship departed.

After they toured Venice a night and day, the ship cruised on to Istanbul and Kusadasi, Turkey. From Kusadasi they were bused a short distance to the ruins of ancient Ephesus before continuing on to Athens to see the Parthenon and further on to Naples, and a visit to the Isle of Capri and the ruins of Pompeii. At the next stop at Livorno in Italy, a motor coach took them to Florence for a day excursion. At Cannes they boarded a train to Monaco and visited the Monte Carlo Casino before concluding the twelve-day cruise at Barcelona. It was a grand cruise marred only by the one-hundred-degree temperature at Pompeii.

Ron had different impressions of each port of call on the cruise. He thought Venice was very romantic. He knew about the canal gondolas, but didn't know the island city was completely pedestrian; motorized vehicles and bicycles were excluded. Away from the crowds it was very quiet and intimate. Istanbul was a city of enigmas; a tour took them to the Holy Hagia Sophia Grand Mosque, the Blue Mosque, the underground cisterns, Topkapi Palace, and the Grand Bazaar with its more than six thousand shops—a buy-and-sell bazaar of myriad items. At Kusadasi, their bus first stopped at the supposed final home of Mary, mother of Jesus, before going on to Ephesus and the site of the tomb of Saint John. Athens was not overly crowded. A tour guide took the group to the Acropolis, on which rests the Parthenon and the Temple of Athena Nike; adjacent to the Parthenon was the Agora ancient market area and the Stoa Museum. Their final stop was at the Plaka shopping district. The town on the Isle of Capri, high up in the midst of the mountains and cliffs, reminded him of Venice because of the romantic intimacy of its apartments and shops. After a very nice lunch in the town of Sorrento, the tour continued on to Pompeii where Mount Vesuvius always loomed over their shoulder.

Florence also reminded him of Venice; vehicular traffic was limited. There were no canals but the Arno River split the city. Its skyline was dominated by the dome of the church of Santa Maria and its bell tower. The next port of call was to be an anchorage off shore at Monte Carlo, but the tender boat ride from the ship to the city was deemed too rough—the only choppy sea on the cruise—so the ship went on to drop anchor at Cannes. They took the train to Monaco and witnessed the everyday ritual of the changing of the guard at the Palace Square and made a brief stop at the casino; it was very nice, but their visit was hurried. Barcelona impressed him, maybe because he didn't know what to expect; it is a cosmopolitan city. A guided half-day tour preceded a walk on the La Rambla, the three-quarter mile long, twenty-yard-wide pedestrian walkway leading from the statue of Columbus near the harbor through a portion of the city. The walkway was bordered on each side by a large market place, restaurants and bookstores separated from the promenade by narrow traffic lanes. On La Rambla Mimes performed among magazine stands, plants, birds and chickens in cages all for sale, yet the walkway did not seem cluttered; it was crowded but still comfortable for walking and people watching. Besides the La Rambla, Gaudi's grandiose Sagrada Familia was a highlight of the city. Under construction since 1882 with a projected completion in the year 2026, it combines Gothic and art nouveau architectural forms. Pope Benedict XVI consecrated the church a minor basilica in 2010.

*Antonio Gaudi's Sagrada Familia
(Holy Family) church in Barcelona*

After the cruise, Ron joined a book discussion group in Columbus started through the local metropolitan library called "Fiction First," but didn't find the books to be very interesting.

Judy arranged another vacation for January 2004, their vacation in paradise. She and Ron had a great time, probably like most everyone else who travels to Hawaii, staying several days each on three of its beautiful islands: Oahu, Kauai, and Maui. Their room on Oahu was at the Royal Hawaiian Hotel (Pink Palace) on Waikiki

Beach. The first day, threatening weather and high winds didn't prevent them from hiking to the top of Diamond Head crater. Predicted rain on Oahu never occurred, and they experienced no bad weather during the eleven days on the islands except for the high winds. After three nights on Oahu, they boarded Aloha Airlines to fly to Kauai, justifiably called the Garden Isle. After renting a car, they drove to their previously reserved Poipu Beach Resort cottage on the south shore and off-loaded luggage. The rest of the day they explored the north shore beaches by car, one of which was used in scenes from the movie *South Pacific*. After the beach excursion, a helicopter tour over the island allowed them to view inaccessible regions such as Waimea Canyon, the Grand Canyon of the south Pacific, and film location for the movie *Indiana Jones and the Raiders of the Lost Ark*. The next three days they visited a coffee plantation, the statue of James Cook—the first white man to visit the islands—and more fantastic beaches including the black sand of Waimea Beach.

Aloha Airlines flew them from Kauai to Maui where a room at the Whaler condominium complex on Kaanapali Beach awaited them, compliments of the storm that brushed Oahu on their first day.

Kaanapali Beach, Maui, Hawaii

The high winds on Oahu created much more damage on Maui, and their original room booking was no longer available. Instead, a ninth-floor room in the condominiums was provided that was much to the liking of Judy. In fact, she claimed it was the best room she stayed in on all of their tours. After a day on the beach, they rented a car and drove to the town of Lahaina to go on a whale watching boat trip. Their last evening, they attended a luau; pork roasted in the ground, with poi and all the trimmings. There were other good meals during the trip, but the food at the luau was the best, except for what Ron called the tasteless poi. Before their late day return flight to Los Angeles, they drove the famous twisting road to Hana to see its black beaches. Their entire time on the islands of Hawaii, high surf signs were posted warning people not to get in the water but it did not bother them. They were not ocean swimmers but did get in the condo pools and waded in the ocean water at most of the beaches.

A May automobile tour to South Carolina and on into Florida was cut short because Ron entered a hospital the night before their planned departure for supposed heart issues that turned out to be stress. After his overnight stay they went to Panama Beach, Florida, for a few days.

In June, Russ, Ron's companion in England, and his family came through Columbus on a driving tour and met him and Don. It had been twenty-five years since he and Russ had been in England. Only able to spend a few hours together, it was still nice to see him and his wife and their two children. Russ worked for a federal agency and he and his family lived in Virginia. In August, Judy found a bargain flight for her sister, niece, and nephew to Atlantic City and included Ron on the weekend trip. Their accommodations were in the Trump Tower hotel and casino. Ron covered all his horse bet losses at the slot machines while the others visited the famous Elephant store in Margate City.

The second week in September, Ron and Judy drove to Bayshore, Long Island, to begin a tour of the Hamptons. It was a fun trip. Parts of Long Island and New York City had record rainfall but they were always driving east on those days and missed all the bad weather. Ron thought the beaches on Long Island rivaled any in Florida, but there were no palm trees and the water was usually only warm during the summer. Their drive took them to Fire Island and Jones Beach, Southampton, Bridgehampton and East Hampton, the lighthouse at Montauk Point, and Sag Harbor. The last full day on Long Island they stopped to watch the horse races at Belmont Park. On the way home, a stop in Philadelphia, visiting Independence Hall and the Liberty Bell and some old row houses built by Benjamin Franklin was enjoyable too.

Ohio was a battleground state for the 2004 presidential elections. Nationwide recounts in the closely contested election were requested, but warned trial cases did not come to fruition. Ron voted for George W. Bush who was reelected for a second term. In November, Ron and Judy celebrated their tenth anniversary.

In 2005 Ron and Judy flew to San Juan, Puerto Rico, in January to begin a second Princess cruise in the Caribbean and their third consecutive cruise onboard the Golden Princess. Judy made all the precruise arrangements for the voyage to Saint Thomas, Saint Kitts, Grenada, the Venezuelan island of Margarita, and Aruba. They did not go ashore for an extended time on Saint Thomas because they stopped there on a previous Caribbean cruise, but on Saint Kitts they went to a nice beach and explored the port town of the village. Ron had read recently that Alexander Hamilton had been born and spent his youth on the neighboring island of Nevis and had often visited Saint Kitts. Grenada, dotted with colorful hillside homes, was still recovering from hurricane damage in some places. They hiked up to the fort overlooking the port, walked through the town and hired a boat to take them across the bay from Saint George's ship dock to the fine Grande Anse beach.

The cruise itinerary indicated a stop at Caracas, Venezuela, but some "trouble" prevented the ship docking there. The captain announced the water level was too low to enter the port, but Ron heard some people had been kidnapped in Caracas not too many days before their visit. Could the low water level have been a ruse so as not to arouse passenger worries? Instead of visiting Caracas, the ship was diverted to Margarita Island, which turned out to have some of the best beaches of all their travels together. Aruba was an island paradise. Upon returning to Puerto Rico, they had enough time to take a day tour into the jungle. All in all, the voyage was fine and the weather could not have been better, but Ron did not think he wanted to go on another Caribbean cruise. A week later Ron was back at work at his job in Columbus.

CHAPTER 11
2005-2010

In February and March, Ron's doctor was frustrated trying to control his high blood pressure. Ron told her a twenty-pound weight loss would probably make a difference. She said, well... ten pounds. Instead of compromising, his loss for the year totaled thirty pounds to a more manageable 170 pounds. A woman at work was successfully using a low-carb diet and Ron began to follow its guidelines too. It worked, but there were digestive issues. Ron could not recommend the plan, but his blood pressure did come down.

February saw the launch of the video streaming website YouTube, which offered instructional tips, music recordings, and sports-related broadcasts along with other video. In April the revered Pope John Paul II died.

Judy continued to work part-time at Macy's and assist the mother of a former co-worker each week. She went on a four-day cruise in April with her sister, niece, and nephew to the Bahamas while Ron attended a retirement seminar at work where he learned that purchased years of service earned with the military, Peace Corps, and the city of Anaheim could be bought to augment a retirement package. It would cost a considerable cash payment to buy what amounted to five years, but he thought it might help him retire earlier. Not long after his purchase the department announced a one-year buyout for people who wanted to retire that year. So, adding his nineteen years of service with The Ohio State University and the state of Ohio to the five years recently purchased plus the one-year buyout from the state meant the retirement criteria of fifty-five years of age with twenty-five years of service had been met. Ron was able to retire almost immediately, effective the end of May. His health had not been good during the year and he thought the opportunity to retire when he did was a gift from God; a most pleasant and welcome event.

In May and June, the thoroughbred horse Afleet Alex won the Preakness and Belmont Stakes. His jockey admitted to guiding the horse on a troubled ride in the Kentucky Derby that led to a third-place finish and prevented the horse from being a Triple Crown winner. Unfortunately, for race fans, the horse never raced again due to an injury later diagnosed as the result of a near fall on his way to the Preakness win. He was retired from racing at the end of the year.

Ron and Judy went on the road in his PT Cruiser through Colorado and New Mexico the last two weeks in August. Ron wanted to go to Rocky Mountain National Park, but Judy had already visited there before they met and was more interested in Taos, New Mexico. Their driving tour took them to both places. In Rocky Mountain National Park, they drove the highest paved road in the United States—over 12,200 feet—and found some fine scenic lakes at the end of several hiking trails. The mountain weather was nice, especially after the extremely hot summer weather in Ohio. After spending time in the park, they exited the west slope and went south to Hot Sulphur Springs, Colorado, to enjoy the mineral baths during an overnight stay.

Leaving Hot Sulphur Springs, they continued their Colorado drive, first stopping at Leadville—the highest incorporated city in the United States, over 10,100 feet—followed by a drive on the Million Dollar Highway from Silverton to Durango. Driving those roads was almost as spectacular as their visit to Rocky Mountain National Park. A two-night stay in Durango had been planned so they could go to Mesa Verde National Park and see its Indian cliff dwellings one day. The next day's drive to Taos and then to Santa Fe preceded their return home. Taos was nice, but Judy and Ron both agreed Santa Fe was a more enjoyable city to visit.

About the time of their return Hurricane Katrina devastated the Gulf Coast, killing over eighteen hundred people. In September, a George Bush nominee, John Roberts, was confirmed as the seventeenth chief justice of the Supreme Court soon after another powerful hurricane, Rita, smashed into Beaumont, Texas. The following month Hurricane Wilma pounded the state of Florida. Even as late as the end of December, a tropical depression named Zeta tied the record for the latest tropical cyclone on record to ever develop in the Atlantic Ocean.

Ron and Judy continued their incredible travel schedule in 2006 beginning with a trip to South America in January. Ron drove his PT Cruiser to Florida and after several days they boarded a Varig Airlines flight to South America. The tour itinerary included stops in Brazil, Iguazu Falls, and Argentina. At their first stop in Rio de Janeiro, Brazil, the beaches were beautiful, the accommodations were first rate, and the weather was great. Iguazu Falls are in the enormous Iguazu National Park that includes tropical jungle land in Brazil, Paraguay and Argentina. The huge falls border the countries of Argentina and Brazil and make up the largest waterfalls in the world.

Iguazu Falls, Brazil, South America

The hotel at the falls was pleasingly rustic and the food was plentiful and delicious. Then it was on to the large cosmopolitan city of Buenos Aires, Argentina, and their hotel in the heart of the city. Ron enjoyed this city more than any of the other destinations. They used the subway to get around, enjoyed a fine dinner show featuring tango dancing, and on one of their self-guided walking tours came across dancers performing the tango on a side street.

Street tango in Buenos Aires

Ron took the subway to the racetrack one night and thought the underground trip was more exciting than the horse races. On another day, a bus took them fifty miles south of the city to the Santa Suzanna ranch where excellent platters of barbecue meats with a dinner were served after a very good horse show. There were other good meals as well. The last day in Buenos Aires they ventured out on their own; a ferry boat transported them across the Rio de la Plata to the historically preserved town of Colonia de Sacramento in Uruguay. As a whole, the trip was much better than expected except for the crowded airline both coming and going. Before returning to Ohio they stayed two nights and relaxed at a Fort Myers Beach hotel. At the end of the month, Samuel Alito, a Bush nominee, was confirmed to be a justice on the Supreme Court.

Through the rest of winter into early spring, things were routine for Ron and Judy. April in New York saw the beginning construction of One World Trade Center's Freedom Tower. In May, he and Judy flew to Las Vegas for a ten-day trip, six days set aside for a national park tour to Utah and Arizona before returning to Las Vegas. The first two days they stayed at the Excalibur Casino Hotel, one night enjoying a Rita Rudnor stand-up comedy show. Rudnor gave Ron a big smile as she walked into the casino theater with her two Afghan hounds. Her show was the highlight of their stay in Las Vegas but did not compare to the natural beauty of the parks: Zion, Bryce, Capitol Reef, Arches, Canyon Lands all in Utah, and the north rim of the Grand Canyon in Arizona. They drove their rented car through other amazing scenery, including the spires and plateaus of Monument Valley. The weather was great too. Judy agreed with a woman she talked to at one stop who said the whole south half of Utah should be designated a national park. They stayed their last two nights in Las Vegas at the Luxor Casino Hotel. Ron cashed in at the slots at the Luxor, winning almost $300. It paid for the Rita Rudnor show and the rental car.

In July the social media platform Twitter was launched, but Ron's tastes were confined to reading books he had accumulated over the years. He was also working in the yard quite a bit, planting some annuals and seeding his small backyard to grass. That same month, Ron, Judy, and her sister drove through upstate New York, stopping at Lake Placid and then at Ben and Jerry's Waterbury Factory and Ice Cream Shop in Vermont, on their way to a town near Bangor, Maine, to visit a cousin-in-law of Judy and her sister before continuing on into the Canadian provinces of New Brunswick and Nova Scotia. It was a very ambitious two-week drive that, in the end, totaled 4,020 miles. Ron and Judy alternated driving her sister's Toyota Corolla, which got very good gas mileage; there was plenty of room for three adults. Some of their stops in Canada included Saint Andrews by-the-Sea, Saint John on the Bay of Fundy, the Hopewell Cliffs, Cape Breton Highlands National Park, Louisbourg and its fortress, Halifax, Peggy's Cove, and lastly Lunenberg. On their return they toured Roosevelt's home at Campobello and drove through Bar Harbor, Maine, next to Acadia National Park, and Kennebunkport. It would not be a trip Ron would want to do again, but they had a good time.

In October, to cut down his driving from Columbus to Bucyrus and back every month, Ron moved his sister from the Bucyrus nursing home to a nursing home in Gahanna, Ohio, a city in the metro region of Columbus and only eight miles from his home. Her forty-year schizophrenia disorder was characterized by her unwillingness to talk or express her feelings. Ron's attempts to get feedback from her on the pending move was useless. Her silence was deafening and at times frustrating but no different from other efforts he made to get her to engage in conversation in the past. However, it wasn't long before it became known she was tolerating much more than the silence she was causing him to endure.

That same month, WikiLeaks, created by Julian Assange, was formed with the purpose to publicize documents from anonymous sources; he has since been indicted in the United States for violation of the Espionage Act. In November, Ron and Judy went on their fourth trip of the year, traveling to Galveston, Texas, for a week. It was not beach weather but self-guided tours through the several historical districts of the city took up most of their time, walking over two miles each day viewing mostly older homes, many predating and some built following the 1900 Great Galveston Hurricane. A subsequent hurricane—Hurricane Ike in 2008—may have greatly damaged some of the many homes built on stilts which was the predominant architectural feature in the city and on the surrounding island. Their condo suite, with a heated pool nearby, was spacious and comfortable during their five nights in Galveston. The last two nights in Houston included a trip to Sam Houston Raceway thoroughbred racetrack one night and a tour of downtown Houston, with a walk through the network of seven-mile-long tunnels that provide an underground connecting pathway for the city. Ron talked Judy into attending two stage productions in Columbus that year: *12 Angry Men* and *The Importance of Being Ernest*. She would have preferred to travel.

In the first half of 2007, Ron's sister was diagnosed with malignant melanoma and passed away in May two days before her sixty-third birthday. The nursing staff at the Gahanna facility conducted a new resident examination and uncovered the tumorous cancer. Her diagnosis was completely unexpected. The melanoma was initially confined to the skin of her vulva. On many of Ron's recent visits to see her he noticed she periodically scratched her genital region and learned later that persistent itching was a side effect of that type of cancer. The staff at the previous facility in Bucyrus apparently did not notice her condition, and Ron thought it nothing more than peculiar behavior. However, an initial exam at Gahanna exposed the cancer and immediate arrangements were made for her hospitalization and surgery. At the hospital, the physician approached Ron in the waiting room with the bad news the cancer had metastasized and was inoperable. It was an open-mouth moment for Ron. His sister's situation should have been detected earlier; she had to have tolerated great pain and discomfort, but never complained or let anyone know how she was feeling. It troubled him greatly to realize his failure to discuss her behavior may have led to the dreadful outcome. If their mother had been alive, his sister's situation would surely not have gone unnoticed.

Overlooked by Ron during the beginning of the year was the election of Nancy Pelosi to be the first woman speaker of the House of Representatives. And the first-generation iPhone was announced by Apple in January prior to its release in April. Two months after the death of his sister, he and Judy decided to drive Judy's Malibu to Virginia, stopping at Monticello and Montpelier, Richmond, the

Colonial Downs racetrack, Williamsburg and historic Jamestown, Virginia Beach, and finally, Onancock; the annual pony swim from Assateague Island to the island of Chincoteague on Virginia's east coast near Onancock was an event they most looked forward to attending. As it turned out, Williamsburg was the best part of the trip. Chincoteague Island was very crowded; it was hot, dirty, and difficult to get close enough to see the ponies swim, although all were herded past Ron and Judy to a sale barn once out of the water.

The last vacation day in Washington was spent walking around the National Mall and touring the Capitol. The new World War II Memorial dedicated the previous year was also nearby.

In September, Ron, Judy, and her sister and brother-in-law traveled to Ireland, taking a ten-day Cosmos bus tour of the country starting and ending near the east coast in Dublin. After two nights in Dublin, they were bused to the west coast town of Sligo, stopping along the way at the Hill of Tara, the historic medieval site of the beginning of the Celtic kingdom. On one day of a two-night stay in Sligo, a motor coach took them into Northern Ireland to the northerly town of Derry and a tour of its old walled city. From Sligo the tour continued on to Ennis, a southerly city, and a stop at Galway Bay to see the Cliffs of Moher. Then it was on to Killarney for two nights. While in Killarney, their bus took them around the southern coastlines of Dingle Peninsula and the Ring of Kerry. The last night was spent in the southeast coastal town of Tramore before returning to Dublin. Much of the country was lined with stone fenced fields and had much lush green pasture that fed countless sheep and cattle. They stopped at more than one pub, a pottery factory, weaving mill, and the Waterford Crystal factory along the way. In Waterville, a statue of Charlie Chaplin was covered due to construction.

Roadside souvenir salesman, near Waterville, Ireland

They had seen a statue of William Yeats—with verse scripted over the entirety of the statue—in Sligo and a reclining statue of Oscar Wilde was near his home in Dublin. Also in Dublin, they saw the ancient Book of Kells at Trinity College and the oft photographed Ha'penny Bridge. Their trip would not have been complete without a stop in County Cork to kiss the Blarney Stone at Blarney Castle. The trip was enjoyed by all. The tour ended in time for Ron to watch the Cleveland Indians lose in the October baseball playoffs. That same month in Minneapolis, the I-35W Mississippi River Bridge collapsed killing thirteen people. Ohio State's football team unexpectedly finished number one in the nation at the end of the year but was soundly defeated by LSU in the BCS championship game.

Ron and Judy continued to travel. Two years earlier they went on four tours, and in 2008 Judy signed them up for three paid excursions and one self-guided trip that accounted for a total of thirty-nine days during the year. The first was a Caravan tour to Costa Rica in mid-January, flying first to the capital, San Jose, for a two day stay. The highlight of the excursion for Ron was a motor boat ride to Pachira Lodge across the river from the Tortuga turtle resort on the coast of the Caribbean Sea. The two-night stay in the remote lodge gave them time to go on several boat outings in search of iguanas, monkeys, birds, and other wildlife. The sea turtles were not laying eggs during their stay, but a few river turtles were sighted. After leaving the lodge, they visited two volcano sites, a hot springs rejuvenation center, both a banana and coffee plantation, and rode atop the jungle on a jump seat. The accommodations and meals were very good; before returning home, they enjoyed a two-night stay at the Doubletree Resort in Puntarenas on the west coast. The weather was an excellent break from the Ohio cold.

After fifty years as president of Cuba, Fidel Castro resigned near the end of February and was replaced by his brother Raul. In April, Danica Patrick won the Indy Japan 300 to become the first woman in history to win an American championship car race. But Judy and Ron were devoting more time to their next trip to Egypt, a nine-day Insight tour. After a long flight they first had a two-night stay at the Marriot Cairo on the bank of the Nile River. It was their base from which the tour took them to the pyramids at Giza, the Egyptian Museum, the mosque at the Citadel of Salah El-Din, and the ancient capital of Memphis, close to Djoser at the Saqqara necropolis where the oldest known pyramid in the world is located.

Djoser pyramid—oldest known pyramid in Egypt, dates to around 2630 BCE

A night train from Cairo to Aswan failed to measure up to Ron's expectations. It was followed by a flight south—with only desert sand in view from the plane—close to the Sudan border to see the rock temple at Abu-Simbel guarded by the huge statues of Ramses II and Queen Nefertari on the western bank of Lake Nassar. In a massive effort, the temple was relocated a distance of two football fields in 1968 due to the construction of the Aswan High Dam. Retuning to Aswan they stayed in the Old Cataract Hotel, made famous by former resident Agatha Christie, before a three day/night Nile cruise. The tour stopped at Luxor to visit the tombs of the Valley of the Kings and other temples before returning to Cairo by air in time to catch another long flight back to the States. The food, weather, and lodging (except for the train) were all excellent. However, Egypt's cities were not clean by Western standards and the hounding hucksters selling merchandise were bothersome at times. Ron remembered the Nile cruise as the best part of their time in Egypt, notable because no one was in their face trying to sell souvenirs.

In May, several notable disasters occurred. The country of Myanmar (Burma) lost 138,000 people, with millions displaced, due to Cyclone Nargis. Ten days later, an 8.0 magnitude earthquake struck Sichuan, China, killing over 69,000 persons.

The death of Ron's Uncle Carroll of a stroke also occurred that same month. Ron never had that close of a relationship with him. He and his wife, his mother's youngest sister, Ron's Aunt Grace, raised their five children in northwest Ohio and it was not convenient for them to visit or be visited that often. However, he knew their youngest daughter, a hair stylist in Columbus. She had cut Ron's hair for almost twenty years. Sometime after Uncle Carroll's funeral, Ron traded his eight-year-old 2001 PT Cruiser for a 2009 Pontiac Vibe, which seems to be a capable vehicle although the gas mileage is not as good as he would like. It has the equivalent cargo space as the PT Cruiser and the same 2.4-liter engine, but the Vibe is a little more stylish. The same month he purchased the car, Ron bought coral-colored carpet roses and planted them in front of his house.

In July, Ron and Judy went to the Canadian Rockies—Banff and Jasper by way of Vancouver. It was his favorite vacation that year. After a long flight, they rented a car and drove a fifteen-hundred-mile round trip starting and ending in Vancouver. The natural wonder of the Canadian Rockies—just as the Colorado Rockies—was spectacular, but not much wildlife was seen—only one black bear, an elk, and a wolf. After a two-night stay in Banff and another night in Jasper they drove to Calgary but it was a disappointing side trip; there was not much to see and it rained that day. Their return drive approaching Vancouver was more scenic, especially because Vancouver Sound was on one side of the highway and spectacular cliffs on the other.

Since his retirement, Ron had been working on an adapted screenplay of a novel, encouraged by Don, who by now had graduated from the American Film Institute with a degree in screenwriting. When Ron told him the novel did not have his preferred ending, Don suggested he write one to his own satisfaction. Completing an adaptation after three years, Ron contacted a story analyst in New York and mailed her a copy for review. She returned the screenplay to Ron with the grim admonishment that "all writing is rewriting." So, Ron began a rewrite. In August Judy sold her house she had lived in for thirty-one years and moved into an apartment. No more lawns to mow or hedges to trim. In September, the first private spacecraft, SpaceX, was launched into orbit. Early in October, President Bush signed the Emergency Stabilization Act passed by Congress. The law created the Troubled Asset Relief Program (bank bailout) so the government could purchase mortgage-backed securities and reinvest them in more stable assets.

Amid all the protests of the bank bailout and the unsure stock market, Ron and Judy left for China and their last tour of the year. After visiting Beijing's Forbidden City and Tiananmen Square, the small tour group was invited to visit a Chinese home located on a quiet pedestrian alley street. Presented to be a typical home, the house was cramped but comfortable and adorned with bird cages and potted plants at its entrance. Later, they were driven to the country to see the Great Wall. Then a flight to the city of Xian with an overnight stay in order to visit the recently (1974) discovered Terracotta Warriors of the ancient Qin Dynasty. From Xian the tour group went to the Lake City of Hangzhou with its green tea plantation, followed by the canal city of Suzhou. The last city on their tour was the most modern city in China, Shanghai. Hundreds of thousands of people from all over China were touring Shanghai but their Globus tour kept them on the move through different areas in the city, including a visit to a school classroom. The tour provided excellent food options and the accommodations were first rate. The weather was good but in Beijing poor air quality created dense city smog. The population of each city the tour visited exceeded the total population of the state of Ohio, impressing Ron as much as any of the tourist sights. The thirteen-hour flights both ways were the only drawback.

In November, Democrat Barack Obama became the first African American in the history of the country to be elected president. His impressive speeches and support secured Ron's vote for his selection over Republican Senator John McCain. Before the month was out, the Dow Jones market index fell to its lowest point in ten years, mainly as a result of the health of the economy due to the bank bailouts. In December a ribbon-cutting ceremony for a home on the near east side of Columbus for people diagnosed with HIV/AIDS and mental health issues took place. It was to be the second house of the Pater Noster ministry in Columbus, devoted to crisis intervention. Ron's donation to NAMI (the National Alliance for the Mentally Ill) on behalf of his sister was intended to be used for a down payment on the very nice ranch-style home. To his surprise, less than six months later it was abandoned. He was informed the donated money had been used to provide food and clothing for the residents in the months before it was closed.

The next year in January, many marveled at the so-called "miracle on the Hudson" when a US Airways passenger jet made an emergency landing on the river after bird strikes disabled both engines; all the passengers and crew survived the landing, and Chesley Sullenberger, the pilot, was properly hailed a hero for the amazing achievement. In March, the financier Bernard Madoff pled guilty in New York to his pyramid scandal in which approximately eighteen billion dollars was swindled from investors.

Judy and Ron embarked on a Cosmos Vacation Tour to Italy in late May. The tour of Rome, the hill country of Tuscany, and the weather, food, and accommodations were excellent and met all their expectations. Rome was outstanding. Besides Rome, they visited the towns of Pisa and Assisi, and while staying at Montecatini in the Tuscan region they were bused on day trips to the towns of Lucca, Vinci, Florence, Sienna, and San Gimignano.

Soon Judy was planning another trip to Europe. This time, a Viking River Cruise from Trier to Nuremberg in Germany. The tour began toward the end of July in Paris. They didn't climb the Eiffel Tower but went to the Notre Dame cathedral; rode a funicular to the hilltop church, the Sacre-Coeur; did walking tours; and Ron spent several hours in the Louvre Museum before joining Judy for a walk through the Tuileries Gardens. After two nights in Paris, a motor coach took them to Luxembourg—stopping at the American Cemetery, the burial site of General Patton —and on to Trier. When the cruise ended in Nuremberg a bus took them to Prague for the last two nights. The weather was not quite as good as Italy in May, the accommodations on the boat were comfortable if not spacious and the food was good, but any deficiencies didn't seem to matter. Paris lived up to all their expectations, and Prague, for which they had no expectations, was grand. But the river cruise departing from Trier, the oldest town in Germany, was even better than the time spent in the cities. The boat passed vineyards covering high hills along both sides of the Mosel River before stopping for wine tasting and a tour in the town of Bernkastel-Kues.

Typical hillside vineyards grow all along the Mosel River valley

Unlike an ocean cruise, land on both sides was always near. The boat cruised the rivers smoothly, even on the swollen Rhine River, docking at Bavarian villages and towns along the way and cruising past many others, each having at least one tall church spire.

Usually when the boat docked at a town, there was a brief tour and then free time to explore at their leisure, or at least until the boat departed. The second day the boat stopped for a tour of Reichsburg Castle at the town of Cochem. Departing Cochem the next night, the boat continued on, docking at Koblenz at the confluence of the Mosel and Rhine Rivers. The next day the boat motored south into the rushing waters of the Rhine River, negotiating the famed Lorelei curve before docking at Rudesheim for a tour of the city. After cruising all night and entering the River Main, the boat stopped at Aschaffenburg followed by a bus ride to Heidelberg for the day, returning to meet the boat at Miltenberg. The next day the boat docked at Karlstadt before crossing the river to Wurzburg, followed by another bus trip, this time to Rothenberg. The final cruise day, they visited Bamberg before docking at Nuremberg and then were bused to Prague to complete the trip with a tour of that city. The Viking River Cruise boat was about one-hundred yards long and carried 140 passengers, in seventy-eight suites. Some suites, like the one Ron and Judy had, were near water level—with two suite decks above their deck and a top deck with lounge chairs; a large dining room was located below decks near the bow. The captain's pilot house was able to be lowered hydraulically, allowing the boat to pass under bridges with low clearance. All told, the boat cruised 280 river miles and passed underneath forty-plus bridges and negotiated numerous locks along the way. Prague was an interesting city. They walked a lot, visited Prague castle, crossed Charles Bridge into the Jewish Quarter, and stopped near the old town square to watch the Astronomical Clock. It remains one of their favorite tours.

In August, President Obama's nominee to the Supreme Court, Sonia Sotomayor, was confirmed as an associate justice.

The following month, their long-awaited trip to Tahiti began. As a young girl, Judy enjoyed the TV show *Adventures in Paradise* and its blond-headed ship's captain. She had wanted to go to the South Pacific for a long time and signed them up for another Princess Cruise aboard the Pacific Princess—850 passengers and crew—from Tahiti to Huahine, on to Rangiroa, Raietea, Bora Bora, Moorea, and back to Tahiti. The cruise didn't completely satisfy her longing because the one island on her most-wanted list to see, Moorea, was the only rainy day of the cruise. She said going back one day might be an option. They had ten fine days in the tropics with warm, humid temperatures, a Princess balcony suite, and all the good food you could eat. Even the twenty-hour one-way travel did not seem bad.

Ron's Uncle Gerald (Max), the husband of the second to youngest sister on his mother's side, died in November at the age of seventy-six. His wife, Ron's Aunt Velma, six children and, at that time, twenty-four grandchildren, and others mourned his passing.

The next January the terrible earthquake in Haiti, killing 316,000 people and destroying the capital city of Port-au-Prince, occurred.

Far removed from that tragedy, a Collette Vacation tour to Kenya, an African country the size of Texas, had already been planned by Ron and Judy for an early February departure, just in time to miss the start of a major snow event in central Ohio; they barely made their connecting flight to Europe because of the weather. It was twenty-five degrees in the afternoon leaving Columbus, seventy-seven degrees in Kenya at midnight the next day. This trip was one of the few Ron initiated, although, as usual, Judy made all the pre-tour arrangements. They traveled to many protected wildlife areas, parks, and preserves great for picture taking and viewing. As their guide said: "Kenya used to be islands of people living in a sea of animals. Today, islands of animals live in a sea of people." At one park or another all the big five animals—lion, leopard, rhinoceros, cape buffalo, and elephant—were seen up close and personal. Also sighted were herds of antelope, including the impala; warthogs; hyenas; wild dogs, which are rarely seen; and just about any other wild African animal. Judy was most impressed with the giraffe.

They stayed one night at the Hotel Fairmont, Mount Kenya, home to an animal orphanage and an animal education center, one of whose founders was the Hollywood actor William Holden. While at the resort they sat on a seat straddling the equator with one foot on the northern hemisphere and the other on the southern hemisphere. After leaving the hotel, they encountered other wildlife including cape buffalo herds that were seen in several places, but on the last two safari days great herds of elephants—more than any the guides had ever seen—upwards of five hundred in several groups were sighted.

Elephant herds, Amboseli National Park, Kenya, Africa

They had photo opportunities of many more elephants congregating in front of the distant snow-covered Mount Kilimanjaro in Tanzania. Prior to the elephant sightings, Ron went on a balloon ascension with several other tourists at one of the parks but saw only one lone elephant while in the air. Later on, hippopotamus foraging in a river came into view. Their guide said he feared the hippopotamus more than any other animal in Africa; he said never get between the hippopotamus and the river.

Another major newsmaker occurred in March when President Obama, who had often stated bipartisanship was an important objective for his administration, signed into law the Affordable Care Act, passed by the Democratically controlled Congress without a single Republican vote. The inability to obtain even one vote from the opposing party as a recognition of bipartisanship was the beginning of Ron's disillusionment with the Obama administration. Representatives and senators from both parties no longer seemed to be working together to craft legislation. In April, the Deepwater Horizon oil drilling rig exploded in the Gulf of Mexico killing eleven workers and created an oil spill that took six months to seal.

Ron and Judy went on a Holland America tour/cruise of Alaska near the end of June. Ohio temperatures were in the nineties upon their departure but in the low fifties when they arrived in Fairbanks. During their twelve days in Alaska, only two were slightly over sixty degrees. After touring Fairbanks, they panned for gold at the El Dorado Mining Company before traveling south by train to Denali National Park. Denali has a large population of animals, including its own big five—caribou, grizzly bear, moose, Dall sheep, and wolf. All were seen at a great distance except the wolf, usually never seen according to their driver, that meandered slowly along the tundra and crossed immediately in front of the bus. Their tour group was among the 80 percent of visitors to the park who never see the 20,322-foot top of Mount Denali, the highest mountain in the United States, due to cloudy bad weather. From Denali they continued by train to Anchorage and then were bused to Seward to board the ship MS Ryndam with a capacity of 1,266 passengers and crew of 560, one of Holland America's many "dam" ships. The ship traveled the inside passage on the voyage, entering Glacier Bay and stopping at Haines/Skagway, Juneau, and Ketchikan before completing the tour/cruise in Vancouver. At Skagway they boarded the White Pass Scenic Railway for a round trip excursion over the nearly 3,000-foot White Pass Summit into Canada's Yukon Territory.

In Juneau they stopped at the Mendenhall Glacier before boarding a float plane for a scenic ride over the glaciers and the surrounding country. Ron was picked to sit in the cockpit passenger seat because his weight mirrored the weight of the pilot.

Float plane view of glacier

At Ketchikan, shopping in several stores consumed much of their time before joining a tour guide to visit several locations frequented by bears that could be watched from a distance. Only a fleeting glance of one bear caught their eye. The guide said the sixty-degree weather was too warm for them to come out.

The nomination of Elena Kagan to be an associate justice of the Supreme Court was confirmed, and she took her seat on the court in August 2010. The Alaska cruise had gone so well Judy signed them up for an Eastern Mediterranean cruise in September with Holland America on the ship MS Westerdam, a midsize ship slightly larger than the Ryndam, with a passenger capacity of nearly two thousand and a crew totaling almost one thousand. They flew to Athens and boarded the ship for its first stops at Istanbul, Antalya, and Iskenderun in Turkey. From Iskenderun, the ship cruised to the port cities of Haifa and Ashdod in Israel. Then it was on to Alexandria, Egypt, and a return to Athens by way of Kusadasi, Turkey, and a return visit to the ruins of Ephesus.

Library of Celsus in background at ruins of Ephesus

Ron and Judy had been to Athens, Istanbul, and Kusadasi before on their Mediterranean cruise but were especially interested in visiting Jerusalem and Alexandria. From Haifa they went to Nazareth and then lunched at a kibbutz next to the Sea of Galilee. From Ashdod the tour took them to Jerusalem and a walk in the old city; the Wailing Wall and the Church of the Ascension were visited, and the golden-sphered Dome of the Rock Islamic shrine was often visible. It was very hot, nearly one hundred degrees, and very crowded on both days in Israel. Alexandria was the most disappointing of all the tour stops; walking several miles through different parts of the city, the dirty, dusty, malodorous conditions were always evident. Ron said it reminded him of other places they visited in Egypt and did not recommend Egypt as a travel destination, with the exception of a Nile River cruise. However, Judy thought Egypt a good vacation destination.

CHAPTER 12
2011-2015

The year 2011 started out on a sour note. On one of the worst snow days of the winter, Judy was cleaning her unsheltered car of accumulating snow, and without warning her feet went out from under her on snow-covered ice that had formed on the sidewalk. She fell hard on her back and lay there for a moment (she may have lost consciousness briefly), then gingerly returned to her apartment. She had broken her back—the thoracic vertebrae between her lumbar disks near the small of her back—but remained at home hoping it was not a serious problem. After two days she asked Ron to take her to the emergency room. X-rays showed the broken vertebrae and prompted a new concern: bone slippage could threaten paralysis if any of the fragments came into contact with her spinal cord. The next day she was transferred to another hospital. Necessary surgery required inserting and connecting titanium bolts to the disks above and below the break. After a ten-day hospital recuperation, and learning to use a back brace, she spent two more weeks recuperating at a nursing home. She continued using the brace until the end of March, and after that wore a magnetic belt four hours each day until the middle of July when she declared herself back to normal.

Several noteworthy events occurred during her rehabilitation. March 15 marked the beginning of the ongoing Syrian civil war. A happier occasion at the end of April was the marriage of Prince William, Duke of Cambridge, to Kate Middleton. At the beginning of May, President Obama announced Osama bin Laden, founder of the terrorist group al-Qaeda, that attacked the World Trade Center buildings in New York, was killed in Pakistan by a squad of Navy SEALs.

Ron and Judy celebrated her recovery by going to Russia for a thirteen-day river cruise, traveling from the city of Saint Petersburg, near the Baltic Sea, onto the Volga River to Moscow with half a dozen other stops along the way. It was very relaxing. The weather was good, as were the accommodations and food, but the best part of the cruise was the cities. In Saint Petersburg, they visited The Hermitage Museum and attended a ballet performance of Swan Lake, after which a motor coach took them to the palace of Catherine the Great and on to the Peterhof Palace and gardens, commissioned by Peter the Great. At one end of Moscow's Red Square, Saint Basil's Cathedral, a beautiful example of Russian architecture, stood next to the Kremlin Wall.

Saint Basil's Cathedral on Red Square

Opposite the Kremlin Wall, the huge GUM department store, both the wall and the store running the length of the square, was another main point of interest.

GUM department store interior

When the tour ended they returned home on the first day of August.

Before long, Judy signed them up for an ocean cruise with many stops in the Adriatic Sea. They departed in mid-October for the two-week Holland America cruise on board the Rotterdam VI, a small cruise ship with capacity of about fourteen hundred passengers and six hundred crew members. Their excellent stateroom had an interior hallway door but also a sliding glass door that opened onto the promenade deck. The cruise started in Athens's port of Piraeus then went on to Corfu in Greece, Dubrovnik, and Split in Croatia. Venice and Ravenna in Italy were the next stops followed by Kotor, Montenegro, and the Greek islands of Crete and Mykonos before returning to Athens. The food and accommodations were very good. The two times it rained weren't a problem.

The first emails Ron received on his new HP Pavilion computer purchased in January 2012 were travel confirmations for a trip to Australia he and Judy had planned the year before. In February they departed for the thirteen-hour flight from Los Angeles to Brisbane and began an almost three-week tour starting in Cairns that proceeded to Darwin and the nearby Kakadu National Forest. From Darwin the tour group flew Qantas Airlines to Alice Springs, one of the many flight miles logged on the tour, and visited Uluru (Ayers) Rock. They departed Alice Springs for Adelaide, taking an almost one-thousand mile, twenty-hour ride on the Ghan train. In Adelaide the tour took them by ferry boat to Kangaroo Island before more air flights took them to Melbourne, Tasmania, and finally Sydney. The summer temperatures ranged from 114 in Darwin to 48 at night in Hobart, Tasmania. Maybe one of the most memorable moments came at an outdoor evening barbecue at Alice Springs when, following a barbecue dinner, they turned off all the lights after dark and the multitude of stars became visible. Though the Southern Hemisphere stars lit up the night sky, Ron thought it not as splendid as the Northern Hemisphere stars he had viewed in the High Sierra Tuolumne Meadows of Yosemite National Park.

In June, Ron's Uncle Russell, his father's youngest brother, died of a stroke at the age of eighty-four. Ron always liked Uncle Russell but never got to spend a lot of time with him. In November, his father's only sister and youngest sibling, Ron's Aunt Evelyn, died at the age of seventy-nine due to a malfunction of her new pacemaker. She and his Aunt Florence, on his mother's side of the family, had been Ron's two primary contacts since the death of his parents. His Aunt Evelyn had emailed Ron the day before, describing a change to a different battery- powered pacemaker at the hospital as a routine adjustment that turned out to be far worse.

In July, Ron and Judy flew to Amsterdam, The Netherlands, for a two-week cruise, primarily to Norway and into the Norwegian fjords. After two nights in Amsterdam, they boarded the Royal Caribbean ship Brilliance of the Seas, a twenty-one hundred passenger ship, for an overnight cruise to the port of Bruges in Belgium. A short bus ride took them into the medieval city for a guided walking tour on the ancient streets and a restaurant lunch. Ron, no longer an imbiber, said he drank the best beer he ever tasted. On the other hand, Judy enjoyed a strawberry-topped Belgian waffle. From Bruges, the ship docked at Le Havre, France, from where they took a day excursion to the island castle abbey of Mont Saint-Michel. The rest of the cruise would take them to several locations in Norway. At the city of Stavenger they were introduced to their first troll (souvenir).

The next stop at Alesund, Geiranger, was at the end of a sixty-mile fjord followed by traversing to its end the longest fjord in Norway, Sognefjord, 124 miles long to the city of Flam. A train from Flam took them up through wonderful mountain scenery nearly three thousand feet to Myrdal station for a waffle and berry lunch before returning to Flam. A final stop at Bergen preceded their return to Amsterdam. It was a very fine cruise.

They flew to Seattle in October for a brief tour of the city before renting a car for a drive down West Coast Highway 101 to San Francisco. It was a ten-day trip and included stops in Olympic National

Forest in Washington, Crater Lake in Oregon—it was seventy-four degrees, exceptionally warm for October—and a drive through several redwood groves in California. They stayed the final two days in San Francisco but the first touring day was hampered by four events that crowded the city—a marathon, music festival and pro baseball and football games. A forty-nine-mile reverse drive through the city to avoid the marathon proved too challenging and spoiled the sightseeing except for a view of the city from Twin Peaks and a stop at the Legion of Honor museum. The second day tour by cable car included Fisherman's Wharf, Chinatown, and Nob Hill. City haze clouded their view of Alcatraz Island and the Golden Gate bridge but the Bay Bridge was visible from Telegraph Hill and Coit Tower.

Hurricane Sandy began causing great damage all along the East Coast of the United States just about the time of their return home. In November, Barack Obama was elected for a second term as president. This time Ron voted for Mitt Romney. The year ended tragically with the Sandy Hook, Connecticut, school shootings that claimed the lives of twenty-eight people.

It was dark and windy in the early morning of January 20, 2013. The winter had been quite mild; it was thirty-six degrees outside, and there was no snow on the ground. Ron was awakened suddenly with an intense thirst at four thirty in the morning and went downstairs to get a drink. Glancing out his kitchen window through the murky night he saw the shadowy figure of a man seemingly fiddling with the lock on his garage door. The man began to move a few steps along the garage and passed through a gap in a property fence into his neighbor's yard, apparently tripping over something and making a considerable noise. Ron waited a few minutes and hearing nothing more was about to return to bed when the motion light on the garage next door detected movement. The man reappeared and strode onto his neighbor's small back deck and looked to be trying to gain entry. Ron called 911 and four police cars came within three minutes; they found the man still trying to gain entry at the back door. An officer came to Ron's house and said the man, an Ohio State student, was drunk and could be charged with public intoxication. End of story? Not quite. His neighbor, who had been burglarized a few months earlier by someone entering his back door, found an iPhone the man had dropped. Meeting with him later, he sold the phone back to the man, which paid all the damages for both a broken window and a damaged back door.

Ron had continued work on an adapted screenplay of a novel since retirement and completed it in 2013. After working on it periodically for almost eight years, he discovered Warner Bros. owned the exclusive rights in perpetuity to the novel; it was the only company he could approach to try and sell the adaptation. Trying to write an original work seemed to be a daunting task, so he wrote a letter to the head of Warner Bros. explaining his revision of the novel with the hope it would be examined. To his surprise, the letter was passed on to Lin Pictures, a subsidiary of Warner Bros. They asked Ron to email the script to them for a review, but in the end, it was rejected. They commented the screenplay was too ambitious for them to consider, probably a kind way to say it was no good.

In March, Pope Benedict XVI, elected in 2005 to replace Pope John Paul II, suddenly retired. Pope Francis was elected to succeed him and he became the first pope from the Americas. The following month people were horrified by the Boston Marathon bombings which took the lives of three people and wounded over 250 more. In the summer Ron took nine very small gold flakes brought back from the Alaska gold mine to a local jeweler. The El Dorado Mining Company, a tourist site where he had attempted to pan for the gold, told him they were worth about $20. He was skeptical, thinking their appraisal might in some way induce people to buy at the mining company shops. But the flakes were confirmed to be gold and Ron cashed them in for $9 after the jeweler took a substantial commission and some other deductions. So, there really is gold in them thar hills.

In mid-August Judy and Ron departed for a trip to Eastern Europe—an Insight tour, Highlights of Eastern Europe. They flew to Budapest for a tour of the city and a dinner cruise on the Danube River before continuing on a seven-city loop bus tour. They stopped at Krakow and Warsaw in Poland, visiting the site of the Auschwitz Concentration Camp between those two cities. After touring Berlin, they stopped in Dresden, Germany. Prague and Cesky Krumlov in the Czech Republic and Vienna, Austria, completed their tour. When they first arrived in Budapest they had to shop for additional clothing because their luggage was misdirected at the airport; it was recovered by the time they arrived at Krakow, which along with Dresden and Vienna they considered the best cities on the tour. Ron went on an abbreviated *The Third Man* tour in Vienna that took him to locations seen in the classic movie. They had been in Prague before but enjoyed returning to the city, this time entertained by a night cruise with hors d'oeuvres on the Vltave River. Unfortunately, a virus struck Ron near the end of the tour that continued to trouble him for the next several weeks.

When they returned home, the company hired to repair the roof on Ron's old garage declared it unsafe and refused to complete the project, so Ron's original plan to build a new garage was back on the table. In December, Ron's Uncle Warren, the last living sibling of his father, passed away at the age of ninety-one. Ron visited him occasionally as he got older and always enjoyed hearing his perspective on different subjects. He had been a bowler when he was younger, finally rolling his only perfect game in a Bucyrus tournament. Unfortunately, that game wasn't enough for him to win; total pins of a three-game set won the tournament and he fell short by a few pins.

Delayed over two months by permit requirements, Ron's old detached garage was finally torn down on the first day of February 2014. Construction of its new replacement began in one of the coldest, snowiest winters on record in Ohio—eighth coldest; second snowiest. Designed by Ron to house a car and work area, a contractor dug a thirty-two-inch deep "L"-shaped trench in the frozen turf, cutting through tree roots after breaking up the cement floor of the old structure. At the bottom of the trench an eight-inch concrete footer was poured to support a block wall laid to ground level, followed by the erection of a wood frame and roof gables. Thick plywood enclosed the building. Vinyl siding—matching the siding on Ron's house—was applied, the roof was shingled, electricity for lighting and a garage opener was added; a cement floor and car entry ramp provided the final touches. Last of all, a white vinyl fence, spanning out from both sides of the garage, was built to shield his property from alley traffic. Persistent bad weather in February and March caused continual interruptions until the work finally ended in the middle of April. Then Ron built a work bench in the new work area and restocked it with his tools and equipment.

New garage and fence

Stress and concern were constant companions of Ron during construction. But when everything was finished, and as the weather turned warm, a new carefree attitude formed in him that seemed to portend an upcoming period of calm and relaxation. The feeling lasted only a few days. Near the end of April, the nearly cloudless sky was delightfully blue and the spring buds had begun to bloom; the sound of birds in the trees filled the air. But while walking briskly along in the midst of his usual daily walk, a simple misstep led to a series of health-related issues. He usually walked on quiet one-way streets facing oncoming traffic as much as possible but many times, as on this day, busy traffic forced him off the street. On what appeared to be an even stretch of the sidewalk, Ron's right foot clipped a barely noticeable protrusion on the walkway. The contact caused him to do a cartwheel and "stick a landing" very hard onto the pavement on his left foot. Pleased not to have fallen, he soon realized, while limping home, his left leg and side were in much pain.

The next two days intense urinary tract pain and accompanying groin pain bothered Ron. On the third day, passing what appeared to be a kidney stone, he called his doctor and was referred to a urologist. Throughout all the next month the groin pain continued. No broken bones or muscular damage was found in X-rays, but in June the urologist performed a cystoscopy, after which a CAT scan was prescribed. All the tests were negative; Ron thought the pain might be nerve-related, and medication he was given seemed to justify his diagnosis because the ache gradually subsided. He also learned during the occurrence his lithium levels were extremely high causing him to have periods of confusion and depression. Whether the lithium readings were the result of these other incidences was never determined.

His health concerns were insignificant compared to the Ebola outbreak that began in January and claimed the lives of over eleven thousand people in Africa over the next two years.

On July 10, nearing their twentieth partnership anniversary, Judy and Ron departed Columbus for a previously scheduled forty-person Globus tour to the United Kingdom. Ron was still not feeling well from illnesses of the previous two months and, coupled with still unidentified high lithium levels, the prospect of a tour was not appealing to him; he almost turned back at the airport and getting on the plane was a struggle as were the next two weeks of the tour. Judy would have had a much better time in London if she had not been looking after Ron. Their second day in the city, Ron went to the hospital in Kensington for medical help, but they could only suggest he use his prescribed medication and get a good night sleep. After two days they left London and traveled by bus, visiting Stonehenge before stopping for two nights in Plymouth. Judy and most of the rest of the tour group went on a day trip to Cornwall the next day but Ron stayed in bed and rested in the hotel room. Then it was on to Cardiff, the capital city of Wales, before arriving at Liverpool, England, with stops along the way in England at Glastonbury, Bath, and Chester. Proceeding into Scotland, overnight visits to Glasgow and Inverness and two nights in Edinburgh were less of a highlight than driving through the Scottish Highlands and viewing Loch Ness. Reentering England, they stayed in York and visited Stratford-on-Avon before coming back to London and then returned home. About one month later, Ron's Uncle Willard, husband of his mother's oldest sister, died on his ninety-second birthday. He and his wife, Ron's Aunt Florence, had been married sixty-five years.

Notwithstanding all the terror around the world, 2015 was fairly routine and predictable for Ron. Judy booked an escorted tour around France in the summer, but Ron decided not to go with her; last year's tour to the United Kingdom had not gone well for him. Because February was the second coldest month in recorded history in the Columbus area, Ron did most of his daily walking at a downtown YMCA. Three days after the first day of spring the last snow fell and by the end of the month the snow was gone and temperatures were on the rise, although the first eighty-degree day did not arrive until May 4. Never a fan of David Letterman's *Late Show*, his retirement in mid-June after thirty-three years as a late-night host had no impact on Ron's viewing preferences.

Before Judy left for her tour of France the political maneuverings had begun in the United States. Hillary Clinton announced her candidacy for the Democratic presidential nomination and Donald Trump was one of several Republicans who announced their run for the White House. Judy returned home the first week in August from an enjoyable tour a month before Queen Elizabeth II became the longest reigning monarch of the United Kingdom at sixty-three years and seven months. While Judy had been gone, Ron was contemplating the different health issues he was facing.

Ron's personal physician had previously referred him to a nephrologist to help bring his blood pressure under control. More recently he was referred to a gastroenterologist for digestive problems. In addition, the psychiatrist who had been so helpful in prescribing Lithium for his bi-polar diagnosis retired; the next several years Ron would be bounced around from one psychiatrist to another for medication management. With all this going on, he began to think of the interrelationships of the many complex functions of the body; how the numerous internal organs work. The illustrations in the reference book *Gray's Anatomy* show all the details of the human body, diagraming interrelations of the organs and different systems. Nine systems of the human body have been identified by physiologists: the immune, digestive, nervous system, circulatory, endocrine, urogenital, respiratory, integumentary and the musculoskeletal system. Eleven systems can be recognized by identifying musculoskeletal as muscular and skeletal, and categorizing urogenital as separate reproductive and urinary systems. Whatever the preferred classification, the interrelationship of these systems and their complexity of functions is mind boggling.

In his neurologist's office while waiting on an exam, Ron examined a wall chart showing the complex, vast network of nerves in the human body. His urologist has a chart indicating the intricate functioning of the urinary system. An enterologist's chart shows interrelated organs of the digestive system—the stomach, large and small intestines, and the colon aided by the operations of the spleen and liver. The respiratory system compels us, in a relaxed state, to breathe air in and out seventeen or eighteen times each minute. If the senses of sight, sound, smell, touch, and taste are factored in, it is even more astonishing how everything works together in the body, not to mention the essential contributions of the brain and spinal cord. Ron understood cells work together to form tissues that form organs that form body systems. The initial breaths of a baby begin a pulmonary cycle of a system of blood vessels that form a closed circuit between the heart and lungs. Taken as a whole, life truly is a miracle.

Just as miraculous are the seed-bearing plants and fruit-bearing trees and animal species that inhabit the Earth. It is difficult for Ron to comprehend the unbelievable coincidence of plants, trees, and animals evolving at just the right time in the right way so as to be available to provide the required sustenance for an evolved human life. It's a theory that could be said to be more implausible than creation. On the other hand, he wondered if evolution could be a form of creation; the single cell had to originate somehow. While thinking about this, Ron remembered that in the Bible, Peter talked about how long ago the heavens were created and the Earth was formed; he wrote, "But do not forget this one thing, dear friends: With the Lord a day is like a thousand years, and a thousand years like a day" (2 Peter 3:8). Ron speculated that by accepting Peter's narrative, years prior to the biblical genealogies could be calculated into the millions.

CHAPTER 13
2016-2021

January 10, 2016, was a record-setting day in Columbus: it was the latest measurable winter snow ever recorded in the city. Meanwhile, Judy and Ron were preparing to go on a previously planned trip to California. The temperatures were unseasonably cool on the trip; many days mirrored the temperatures in Ohio. They had never stayed in Death Valley, so their planned trip was to be from Los Angeles to Death Valley by way of Lone Pine, California, and Las Vegas, returning to Los Angeles by way of Joshua Tree National Park and Palm Springs. They made advance reservations at the Furnace Creek Ranch and Resort in Death Valley and for an AAA car rental. Santa Monica, the starting and ending point for their driving tour, did not have beach weather when they arrived; walking tours and a visit to the pier filled their time. Going on to Santa Barbara, a visit to its historic mission preceded their drive to Lone Pine from where they viewed Mount Whitney, the highest mountain in the continental United States at 14,505 feet. Their two nights at Furnace Creek in Death Valley was located a short distance from Badwater Basin.

Badwater Basin, Death Valley, California

The basin, at 282 feet below sea level, is the lowest elevation in the United States. The nights were cold in Death Valley with thirty-two-degree temperatures—the lowest- ever temperature in Death Valley was fifteen degrees in January, 1913. Interestingly, the highest-ever temperature was 134 degrees in July of the same year. After leaving Furnace Creek, they stopped in Las Vegas, traveled through Joshua Tree National Park on the way to Palm Springs, and then returned to Santa Monica and temperatures in the low eighties on their last day.

On June 3, boxing legend Muhammad Ali died at the age of seventy-four. That same day, Judy and Ron left Columbus and traveled to Spain for a twelve-day Insight tour, considered an easy-pace tour starting in Spain's second largest city, Barcelona, on the shore of the Mediterranean Sea. From Barcelona, the tour traveled north to the Atlantic coast resort city of San Sebastian and finally to the capital city, Madrid. They were in each city three days and had optional day trips along the way. The day trips included stops at Pamplona, famous for the running of the bulls; the Guggenheim Museum located in Bilbao; and the ancient city capital of Toledo. They also went on an excursion to nearby Biarritz on the Atlantic coast of France one day.

After their return near the end of June, the United Kingdom shocked many in the world by voting to withdraw from the European Union. In July, Hillary Clinton became the first female nominee to be president of the United States. She would lose in a close election—winning the popular vote—to businessman Donald Trump. Ron voted for Trump.

Earlier that summer, Judy went on a solo tour through Germany. Meanwhile, Ron and Jeff, his former boss, continued to occasionally visit Ohio race tracks together, including Belterra Race Track and Casino in July and August. Both those times at Belterra they made it a double header by going to a Riverfront Stadium night baseball game to watch the Reds play. In November the Chicago Cubs ended a 108-year World Series drought by beating Cleveland in seven games, the seventh game ending in extra innings as did the 1997 World Series that Cleveland lost to Miami. With its win, Chicago ceded to Cleveland the longest ongoing record of not winning the World Series; the Indians had gone sixty-eight years at the end of that season without a championship.

The year 2017 produced its usual amount of ups and downs. It began with a quiet winter at home but domestically the political fallout of the election of Republican Donald Trump was already beginning. On the day of his inauguration, a Washington Post newspaper headline read "The campaign to impeach President Trump has begun." The day after his inauguration a network of women marches in Washington and six hundred other cities around the world, estimated to total five million people, took place. The marches were politically organized to advocate for women's rights and other issues, prompted by alleged anti-women remarks by the new president. The first proposed article of impeachment was made by a Democratic congressman in July after President Trump dismissed FBI Director James Comey.

The dismissal of Comey led to the appointment of Robert Mueller as special counsel to investigate Trump campaign collusion with Russia in the 2016 election. Many of the calls for impeachment were ignored because of a Republican-controlled House of Representatives, but things changed when the midterm elections turned control of the House to Democrats. The indignation of the Democratic party was also apparent when a Trump Supreme Court nominee, Neil Gorsuch, was confirmed as an associate judge the first week of April. The confirmation filled a vacancy on the court following the death of Antonin Scalia that had been held open by a Republican-controlled Senate for over a year, denying an Obama nominee a vote.

Amid all the political turmoil, Ron's Aunt Kathryn died at age eighty-nine. The wife of his Uncle Jim who had passed away in 1969, she never remarried, outliving her husband by forty-eight years. Attending the funeral services in Upper Sandusky were her four sons and three sisters-in-law, the younger sisters of Ron's mother.

Toward the end of May, Ron and Judy embarked on an American Queen Mississippi River boat cruise from New Orleans to Memphis. Ron organized the disappointing cruise. Arriving a day early, they roamed around the French Quarter. Ron also visited the National World War II Museum. Once on the boat, high waters prevented it from stopping at two prime locations—Oak Alley and Francisville. They had stopped at those places on a previous driving tour but would have enjoyed visiting them again, arguably the two best stops on the cruise. Instead, the boat stopped at Baton Rouge, a city they were not eager to visit again. The other stops, Vicksburg, Natchez, and Helena, Arkansas, fell short of expectations too. In Natchez, Judy fell down hard on some steps. Ron thought it a wonder she didn't break her back again but she was fine. Even cruising on the river was a bust as there was hardly any boat traffic and only tree-lined banks on both sides of the swollen river with no visual breaks. To cap it all off, Judy got a bad cold the last two days and had to stay in bed and when the tour ended, after returning to Columbus by rental car, Ron became ill for the next month.

In August, Cleveland's baseball team began a winning streak of twenty-two games that now stands as the longest- ever win streak in the American League and second only to the twenty-six-game streak by the 1916 New York Giants. Sad to say the Tribe lost in the playoffs. Near the end of August, Judy and Ron went on a Northern Scandinavian Capitals tour arranged by Globus. The bus tour started in Copenhagen, capital city of Denmark, and continued on to Oslo, Stockholm, and Helsinki, capital cities of Norway, Sweden and Finland respectively, with a day tour to Tallinn, capital city of Estonia. This was a much better tour than the Mississippi River cruise. The weather was fine as were the accommodations and the fellow travelers. All the cities had their own unique features but Tallinn's old city was probably the highlight as were the several water passages by ferry. Both Judy and Ron got ill again after this tour, an unwelcome occurrence on their travels of late.

In October, the deadliest mass shooting by an individual occurred at a Las Vegas Route 91 Harvest music festival by a gunman shooting from a thirty-second-floor room of the Mandalay Bay Hotel. Sixty people were killed, over four hundred wounded and countless more injured in the ensuing panic.

Judy and Ron did not travel in 2018; Ron thought his traveling days might be over. Starting in July, Judy had been shuttling back and forth from Columbus to Dayton for several days each week to stay with her sister and brother-in-law. Her sister had turned seventy and in the last few years had developed a degenerative disorder, scleroderma. She had also recently fallen and suffered a compression fracture in her back. Ron's year started off fine, but the spring brought a whole set of problems. His sleep was disturbed one night by a raccoon on the porch roof outside his bedroom window trying to rip up the rubber roofing, presumably to find a place to raise her babies. She was not successful but moved higher up to a chimney opening that never had a cap or guard on it for the thirty years he had lived in the house; in all that time no creature had attempted to make a home in the chimney. Ron called a wildlife control company. It trapped the raccoon plus five more, twelve opossum, and one groundhog. The bill was slightly less than the cost to install a chimney guard and do other chimney repairs.

In May, media attention of the marriage of Prince Harry, Duke of Sussex, to the American actress Megan Markle dominated the airwaves. In June, President Trump met with North Korean Chairman Kim Jong-un in Singapore, the first-ever meeting of leaders of those two countries. At Ron's home, a different kind of meeting took place when, after returning to bed after a middle of the night bathroom trip, his eye caught sight of an unusual looking bug crawling on the sheet. He brushed it off, but when it happened again the next night a search on the internet confirmed his suspicion that he had bedbugs. Somehow the disgusting creatures got into his house and took up residence in a burlap-covered bed platform and headboard he had constructed years earlier. He called an exterminator and in the process of their work a couch became his bed for a month. Fortunately, the infestation was isolated to the burlap, which he promptly removed from the house.

By the end of July, Ron had symptoms of fatigue and an intestinal disorder that preceded an undefined illness. His doctor did some lab tests and referred him for a CAT scan, an MRI, and then a colonoscopy. Nothing related to any intestinal issue was found, but a microcyst discovered on the pancreas was cause for concern. It took him over a month to feel better from the illness that he blamed on yet another insect. He was in his backyard one day and started to swat a small mosquito perched on his forefinger when it gave him a painful poke. Everyone who heard his suggestion was skeptical it could have caused Ron's problems.

To put things in perspective, his illness did not approach the catastrophic damage and humanitarian crisis Puerto Rico suffered in August as a result of hurricane Maria. In October, Brett Kavanaugh, the Trump nominee for associate justice to the Supreme Court, denied allegations during the last day of the confirmation process of sexual assault that was said to have occurred forty years earlier. The claims could not be proved and the nominee was confirmed by a narrow margin to replace retiring Justice Anthony Kennedy.

In March 2019 Robert Mueller's two year-long investigation concluded that Donald Trump's campaign did not collude or conspire with Russia during the 2016 presidential election. However, an ongoing John Durham investigation has since indicted several Clinton campaign operatives who may have provided false information to the FBI concerning Russian collusion. The Mueller conclusion did not deter the newly elected Democratic-controlled House of Representatives from impeachment proceedings later in the year by claiming Trump broke the law by soliciting help in a telephone call to a foreign government leader. They claimed Trump was trying to get material damaging to Joe Biden, his political rival. The Republican-controlled Senate later acquitted Trump of the impeachment charges.

In April, the world watched as the 850-year-old Notre Dame cathedral in Paris was decimated by fire. Efforts to restore the building as it once was still continue.

Except for two major projects, the year was dominated by Ron's health issues. Last year ended with his recovery from a gastrointestinal issue that was never diagnosed. He had discontinued his daily two-to-three-mile walks but early in the year shorter walks on uphill climbs caused chest pain. He contacted his doctor thinking it was the return of the gastro problem from the previous year. To be safe, his doctor thought a best first step would be a referral to a cardiologist; it turned out Ron had coronary artery disease. The cardiologist found a 90 percent blockage in his left coronary artery and two 80 percent blockages in the right artery. Stents were placed in the arteries, and he was told his normal life span would not be reduced by the inserts. Ron thanked his doctors for helping him avert a problem that could have been much worse.

Ron had difficulty adjusting to several new prescribed medications after the artery procedure. In order to use expected new blood pressure medications that had contraindications to Lithium, he agreed to end his twenty-six-year management with that drug and switch to another bipolar medicine. His concern as to the efficacy of the new treatment proved to be baseless; it turned out to be just as effective as Lithium.

Because of these new treatments, several home projects were put on hold for several months. In June he hired a landscaper to clean up his small backyard. They hauled out over a dozen concrete slabs butting up against the back of the house, seeded the area with grass, and cut down a cedar tree at the front of the house that had grown excessively tall. In addition, his property fence was repositioned.

The next project began a month later when a dimmer switch fell out of the living room wall. The electric wiring in the old house was knob and tube. While trying to repair the dimmer switch by himself, Ron detected an electrical odor and thought it was time to hire a contractor to rewire the house. They completed the job in five days. Now the wiring was up to code, wireless smoke detectors have been installed, and even the dimmer switch was repaired. They were fast, thorough, and expensive.

In September, Ron completed a three-month cardio lab at an Ohio State rehab facility and, using a Silver Sneakers program, joined a fitness club. But soon his gastrointestinal problems returned. His gastroenterologist thought the cyst on the pancreas might be the cause, but another MRI showed the micro-sized cyst had not changed or expanded. However, his gastro issues continued to mid-November about the time he and Judy celebrated twenty-five years together. Much to her regret, their yearly travels have been curtailed due to Ron's health issues.

Even with all his recent health problems, Ron hoped to self-publish a novel he had worked on for over four years after failure to succeed with his screenplay. The book, expected to be ready by the end of the year, is about a corrupt Australian politician and the despicable actions he takes in an election year. Ron signed a contract with Luminare Press, an Oregon publishing firm, to guide him through the self-publishing world and was very pleased with their help and expertise. It is a paperback book—about 165 pages, available on Amazon with an e-book distribution.

Two significant happenings occurred at the beginning of the year 2020. Ron's published novel, *Elusive Getaway,* became available on Amazon at the end of January just about the same time the coronavirus was detected. These two unrelated events had different outcomes. The coronavirus spread worldwide while his book slipped into obscurity.

The pandemic changed his habits and the routines of several of his friends. By late spring, a weekly dinner with Don, Keith, and Jeff became an outdoor event at a reservoir park and continued throughout the summer when dining indoors was discouraged and then prohibited. When the weather prevented them from getting together outside, they began to meet using a teleconference program. Jeff was the brains setting up their computer virtual meetings.

Ron's Aunt Florence, his mother's oldest sister, died the first week of March at the age of ninety-one. After his parent's deaths in 1996 and the death of his Aunt Evelyn, she had been Ron's primary family contact. They talked by phone during the year, and if his travels took him to the Bucyrus area he often stopped at her home and engaged in lively talks concerning such things as herbal supplements, gardening, and politics—especially concerning politics. The last year before her death she had been living in an assisted- living facility before entering a nursing home.

Following the death of Justice Ruth Bader Ginsburg in September, Amy Coney Barrett, President Trump's third nominee to the Supreme Court, was confirmed by a narrow vote, controversially scheduled one week before the 2020 presidential elections by a Republican-controlled Senate.

Besides Ron and his friends meeting during the year, the dining habits of Ron and Judy also changed because of the pandemic;

carry-out and home cooking replaced restaurant dining. Judy, always a book reader, began working on jigsaw puzzles when not commuting between her home to be with her sister and brother-in-law during the week. Ron's lifestyle was not affected greatly by the coronavirus, but other health issues, particularly related to his digestive tract, were a concern. In June an endoscopic ultrasound found an H. pylori bacterium in his stomach and detected celiac disease in the small intestines. Antibiotics took care of the bacteria but a gluten-free diet had to be followed to combat the disease. The diet has helped but his grocery bill is 15 percent higher.

Ron had never heard of celiac disease before the diagnosis. He learned it can occur as a person gets older and sometimes following surgery. His Aunt Velma theorized genetically modified grains may be causing more and more people to have gastrointestinal issues. Before his coronary artery surgery last year, digestive issues were probably indicating something was changing in his body. It was his only explanation for the onset of celiac disease unless medications used in his surgery somehow triggered the ailment. A gluten-free diet required, among other things, no ingestion of wheat, barley, or rye-based foods. Rice and oat products became alternative food choices. However, his digestive problems continued even after initiating the diet. By doing research, he found one of his heart medications was wheat-based. Once that medication was discontinued, he began feeling better.

In February, Ron had his basement waterproofed and a sump pump installed and later hired a contractor to replace the old cellar steps and install a handrail. The new steps will make it more comfortable for him to use an inflatable hot tub he purchased and set up in the basement to help to warm his cold feet and legs—diagnosed as neuropathy.

At the end of July, a huge tree limb fell from an elm tree in Ron's backyard. He got up one morning to discover it had opened a small hole in his neighbor's garage roof, pulled down power lines in back of the house and completely blocked the alley. The city cleared the alley, the electric company shut off and later restored power so an electrician Ron hired could repair the damages. Ron's homeowner's insurance paid for most of the electrical repair work, less a deductible. His neighbor was able to easily repair the damage to his garage roof.

Besides the coronavirus and political dissension between the parties, racial injustice heightened by the killing of George Floyd in Minneapolis dominated much of the news. His death spawned many protests and rioters across the nation, particularly in Oregon and Washington State. Joe Biden was elected president in November much to Ron's disappointment, but he wishes him good luck and good governing. Ron thought Trump was his own worst enemy, continually responding to media reports via Twitter although, with over 90 percent negative reporting by major news media outlets, Ron could understand the frustration of the soon-to-depart president.

In the second week of December, Ron had new shingles put on the house. The same company that repaired the roof twenty-seven years ago—with twenty-five-year shingles—did the job; it was past time for new ones. The cost of the work increased by only 65 percent in all those years. He also purchased a new HP desktop computer to replace the one he used for nine years. He thought it would help in teleconferencing, but transferring data from one to the other was a challenge.

Ron had been reading the Bible daily for several years and was inspired by scripture from time to time. After asking Jesus Christ into his heart forty years earlier, he was still trying to accept by faith God's forgiveness of sin by grace through belief in his son Jesus Christ. Faith is mentioned often in the Bible: we are sanctified, justified, and made righteous by faith; we can walk in faith and have access to grace by faith. But the Bible also says God is faithful (Psalm 33:4): "For the word of the Lord is right and true; he is faithful in all he does."

January 6, 2021, was a dark day for the country as rioters stormed the United States Capitol building protesting the outcome of the 2020 presidential race. Before Joe Biden took office, President Trump, in an attempt to change the outcome of the electors, continually claimed election fraud and initiated many court litigations. His efforts were all denied and the new president was sworn into office on January 20. Meanwhile, the former president was impeached by the House of Representatives a second time in February after they adopted one article stating he was involved in the incitement of insurrection arising from the January 6 assault. Once again, the Republican- controlled Senate acquitted Trump of the charges. Ron did not believe Trump intentionally set out to incite the rioters. His speech on January 6 was no different in many ways than several campaign rally speeches Ron had heard him deliver throughout the year, but his persistent objections after the election would have probably been better confined to the courts. Ron's initial good impressions of Trump faded as they had with President Obama, but for much different reasons. Obama's policy views irked Ron; he appreciated many of the courses of action of the man who succeeded Obama but came to dislike Trump's continual abrasive personality.

Vaccines rapidly developed when Trump was in office, designated as Operation Warp Speed, provided immunity to the coronavirus and were given emergency use authorization just before the new year; many individuals began to receive the injection. Even though Ron was qualified to receive the vaccine as early as February, his first injection was delayed until late April because of his concern a vaccine ingredient might have caused an earlier allergic reaction. After seeing an allergist, it was determined his concerns were unfounded. Being able to teleconference allowed him to keep in touch with Don, Keith, and Jeff in the winter, but he and Judy continued to meet regularly.

Judy continued to stay several days at a time for many weeks with her sister and brother-in-law, commuting from her Columbus home to Dayton. In June her sister took a sudden turn for the worse and within two weeks mercifully died at the age of seventy-two.

The onset of the disease scleroderma, which wracked her body, had left her almost incapacitated. Her sister-in-law's husband died the following month at the age of seventy-nine.

President Biden concluded the war in Afghanistan at the end of August, but his controversial withdrawal of American troops and citizens, and Afghan allies led to chaos and the death of thirteen American service personnel. That decision and the continued rise of the delta and omicron variances of the coronavirus has caused his once high approval ratings to weaken considerably. In addition, the southern border separating the United States from Mexico was overrun with Haitian refugees after an earthquake in that country, causing even more problems for the Biden administration. The recent passage of a bipartisan infrastructure bill may improve the president's standing among the electorate.

The conclusion to the year 2021 brings to an end the over one-hundred-year Cleveland baseball team nickname, Indians. Beginning in 2022 the baseball franchise will henceforth be known as the Guardians, but the change was not without controversy and embroiled the team in a legal dispute with the Cleveland flat track roller derby team that had previously adopted that nickname. Legal maneuvers were hinted at by the roller derby founders but the outcome was settled and both parties have agreed to use the same designation; Guardians will be the nickname of both teams.

At first, Ron was disgusted a nickname change was being considered. He could not understand how the nickname Indians could be offensive. Likewise, he believed the appellation "Tribe," also used in conjunction with the team, did not project any negative connotation. He supposed a headline saying, for example, "the Tribe was on the war path," could be viewed acrimoniously but rarely had he heard that phrase or saw it in print. To Ron, the name change was symbolic of loud minority voices clamoring for political correctness. But lately he has had to reconsider his point of view: Indians, thought to be an identification coined by Christopher Columbus, is considered by Native Americans a pejorative term applied to indigenous people by white Americans. With that in mind, he has begun to understand the reason for a change. However, he thinks "Rockers"—Cleveland is the home of the Rock & Roll Hall of Fame—would have been a better choice.

As Ron surpasses his seventy-fifth birthday in 2022, he wanted to bring the memoir to an end, at least for now, by thanking God for all the people in his life who helped him along the way, beginning with his parents and sister. Many others are also deceased, including Billy Graham, the teacher at Teen Challenge, and the psychiatrist who diagnosed his condition and managed his medication for many years. He has lost track of other people, many of whom he undoubtedly hurt by promoting his own self-interests and ignoring their personhood, but he still corresponds with a former Peace Corps volunteer and receives Facebook posts from cousins and friends. He feels blessed to have been able to maintain friendships with Keith and Jeff for almost thirty years and Don, his friend from their days together in school, for fifty-five years. Most important has been his long partnership with Judy and his growing love for her.

As Ron continues to examine the Bible, the statement "the love of Christ, and to know this love that surpasses knowledge" (Eph 3:18, 19) is instructive by its spiritual declaration. The verse expresses the idea that it is impossible for human beings to comprehend what God did for us when he sacrificed Christ on the cross and his blood was shed so our sins could be forgiven; it cannot really be understood but is a mystery that has to be accepted by faith. "Now faith is being sure of what we hope for and and certain of what we do not see (Hebrews 11:1). The rest of Hebrews chapter 11 has much more to say about faith and how the ancient people were commended.

Finally, Paul writes in his letter to the faithful Romans (5:1, 3): "Therefore, since we have been justified through faith, we have peace with God through our Lord Jesus Christ, . . . Not only so, but we also rejoice in our sufferings, because we know suffering produces perseverance; perseverance, character; and character, hope. And hope does not disappoint us, because God has poured out his love into our hearts by the Holy Spirit, whom he has given us."

All quoted scripture is from the New International Version of the Bible.

www.ingramcontent.com/pod-product-compliance
Lightning Source LLC
LaVergne TN
LVHW021718060526
838200LV00050B/2726